Marketing and Promoting Electronic Resources: Creating the E-Buzz!

Technological advances allow libraries to more readily serve patrons' needs. But how can a librarian effectively communicate what services libraries offer? *Marketing and Promoting Electronic Resources: Creating the E-Buzz!* explains the foundations of marketing and promotion, focusing on practical and creative techniques that have worked in academic, public, and special libraries. Respected authorities from various libraries offer their insights and advice for effective marketing strategies for electronic resources such as e-serials, databases, and e-books, helping library patrons to better understand the resources now available to them.

This book provides librarians with practical suggestions on how to best let their patrons know about the available e-resources and instruct them on how to use them effectively. Librarians in any type of library setting, even if previously unschooled in marketing campaigns, can find fresh ideas to apply in their own setting. This invaluable tool discusses in detail how to develop a marketing plan, create and finance a promotional campaign, and how to use new technologies to reach out to your library patrons in the most effective way to promote your e-resources.

This material was published as a special issue of *The Serials Librarian*.

Eleonora Dubicki is an Assistant Librarian, at the Monmouth University Library in West Long Branch, NJ. As a librarian, she has been responsible for collection development for electronic resources, and reference and instruction in academic and special libraries. Before coming to Monmouth, she worked as a Market Analyst for Telecordia and Lucent. Her work has been published in Technical Services Quarterly and she has written a chapter in Usage Statistics of E-Serials. She holds an MLS from the School of Communication, Information, and Library Studies at Rutgers University, and an MBA from Rutgers Business School – Newark.

D0145335

Marketing and Promoting Electronic Resources: Creating the E-Buzz!

Edited by Eleonora Dubicki

Routledge
Taylor & Francis Group
LONDON AND NEW YORK

First published 2009 by Routledge
2 Park Square, Milton Park, Abingdon, Oxon, OX14 4RN

Simultaneously published in the USA and Canada
by Routledge
270 Madison Avenue, New York, NY 10016

Routledge is an imprint of the Taylor & Francis Group, an informa business

Typeset in Times by Value Chain, India
Printed and bound in the United States of America on acid-free paper by IBT Global.

British Library Cataloguing in Publication Data
A catalogue record for this book is available from the British Library

ISBN10: 0-7890-3585-5 (hbk)
ISBN10: 0-7890-3586-3 (pbk)

ISBN13: 978-0-7890-3585-1 (hbk)
ISBN13: 978-0-7890-3586-8 (pbk)

Marketing and Promoting Electronic Resources: Creating the E-Buzz!

CONTENTS

Introduction

One of the most significant trends that has occurred in libraries over the past two decades is the dramatic impact of technology and the resulting shift from print materials to electronic resources (e-resources) such as e-journals, aggregator databases, and ebooks. Technology and access to the Internet have changed the basic techniques for accessing information and conducting research. Furthermore, technology has also created new tools for libraries to communicate with users—e-mail, Web sites, blogs, instant messaging, and RSS feeds.

A trip to the library is no longer mandatory to conduct research. Users are increasingly accessing information from their homes, offices, or schools. Nancy Davenport states that "today's information-seekers get much of what they need electronically, often far from the physical library."[1] As a result, users see libraries and librarians in a different perspective. Judith Siess suggests, "Information at the desktop is no longer necessarily connected to a library or librarian in the user's mind. We are becoming more and more 'invisible.'"[2]

WHERE DO USERS GET INFORMATION?

According to a 2005 OCLC report, libraries are not the first place users turn to find information—"84% percent of information searches begin with a search engine."[3] In fact, most users are not aware if their libraries provide access to electronic journals and "the majority of information seekers are not making much use of the array of electronic re-sources (online magazines, databases and reference assistance, for example) libraries make available to their communities."[4] A 2006 PEW Internet and American Life Project survey found that 73% of Americans currently access the Internet.[5] Library patrons are accustomed to the quick access to information provided by the Internet. Patron research habits have undergone dramatic changes–gone are the days when patrons came into the library to use print materials, including indexes to find citations, and then went to bound journals or microfilm to get the full-text copies of articles. Today's library patrons expect easy access to electronic information and are more likely to self-serve. However, conducting research can be overwhelming–thousands of items are retrieved from an Internet search. Resources that once had restricted access are now available electronically. Enter the librarian–an expert to train users to access the best information in an efficient manner. Librarians still strive to provide patrons with the "right" answers. Quality has always been important to us, and therefore the widespread access to Internet information, authoritative or not, has directed our efforts to teaching evaluation of sources and how to access the authoritativematerials libraries offer. With these changes in conducting research, libraries can no longer fully meet current patron needs with print-only materials and limited access hours–they need to offer e-resources. The library has now become widely accessible electronically, and the library's Web site serves as an additional entry point to the library and its resources. Patrons can access information remotely at anytime from anyplace.

EXPENDITURES

Libraries are spending more and more money on purchasing materials in electronic format. According to the Association of Research Libraries (ARL), the percentage of the average academic research library budget spent on e-resources increased from 3.6 percent in 1992-93 to 37 percent in 2004-2005. ARL university libraries reportedly spent almost $330 million on e-resources in 2004-2005.[6]

Public libraries and school media centers have also experienced growth in access to the Internet and e-resources. Results of a 2006 public library survey show that 98.9 percent of public libraries are connected to the Internet, and 36.7 percent offer wireless Internet access.[7] The National Center for Education Statistics (NCES) estimates that there were 170, 782 Internet terminals in public libraries, and e-resources usage levels reached 343 million in 2004.8 NCES also estimates that expenditures for collection materials in electronic format were one percent of the $8.6 billion total FY2004 operating expenditures for public libraries.[9] School media centers are providing elementary and secondary school students with access to databases. Seventy-five percent of media centers provided access to databases, with 44 percent offering 1-3 databases, 14 percent offering 4-6 and 17 percent 7 or more.[10]

Similar to increased costs for print materials, the costs for e-resources also continue to rise, and libraries must validate the expenditures for these products. The rapid growth in the number of e-resources calls for the library's commitment to promoting these resources and providing efficient access to these research tools.

CHALLENGES FOR LIBRARIES

How do users find out about e-resources? According to the OCLC study,[11] 61 percent of users learn about e-resources from friends. Links from Web sites of electronic information sources were used by 59 percent of users, and promotions and advertising led 39 percent of users to additional e-resources. Less than 20 percent of users discovered new e-resources from librarians or teachers. In fact, users are generally confident in their research skills and are happy to self serve–"Most library users say they have not asked for help using any library resources, either at the physical or the virtual library."[12] Clearly, we are not doing an effective job of reaching out to patrons to inform them of the e-resources available from the library.

The challenge for librarians to is create an awareness about e-resources and to stimulate stronger usage. "A successful long-term library marketing campaign will be able to differentiate the library's focus and services from the variety of information services and electronic resources offered on the Web."[13] Librarians need to embrace marketing–understanding our patrons and their needs, and communicating to them the e-resources we offer to address those needs.

The focus of this book is developing effective marketing programs and promotional campaigns to create a buzz about e-resources. The chapters are written by librarians who have developed and implemented marketing and promotional campaigns in their libraries. The goal of this book is to provide libraries with proven marketing and promotion techniques which have been used successfully to improve awareness of e-resources and can serve as models for creating your own library's marketing program.

Eleonora Dubicki

REFERENCES

1. Nancy Davenport, "Place as Library?" *Educause Review, 41* (January/February 2006): 12.

2. Judith A. Siess, *The Visible Librarian Asserting Your Value with Marketing and Advocacy* (Chicago: ALA, 2003), xiii.

3. OCLC, *Perceptions of Libraries and Information Resources,* (Dublin, OH: OCLC Computer Library Center, Inc, 2005), 1-17. *http://www.oclc.org/reports/2005perceptions.htm* (accessed October 6, 2006).

4. Ibid, 6-4.

5. Mary Madden, "Internet Penetration and Impact" PEW Internet & Data Life Project, Data Memo, April 2006. *http://www.pewintemet.org/pdfs/PIP_Intemet-Impact.pdf* (accessed October 6, 2006).

6. Martha Kyrillidou and Mark Young, *ARL Statistics 2004-2005*, Association of Research Libraries, *http://www.arl.org/stats/pubpdf/arlstat05.pdf* (accessed November 21, 2006).

7. John Carlo Bertot and others. *Public Libraries and the Internet 2006: Study Results and Findings.* (Tallahassee, FL: Inforrnation Use Management and Policy Institute, Florida State University, 2006), 1. *http://www.ii.fsu.edu/plintemetreports.cfm* (accessed October 6, 2006).

8. Adrienne Chute and others, *Public Libraries in the United States: Fiscal Year 2004* (NCES 2006-349) U.S. Department of Education, National Center for Education Statistics (Washington, DC:National Center for Education Statistics, 2006) *http://nces.ed.gov/pubs2006/2006349.pdf* (accessed October 6, 2006).

9. Ibid.

10. Leslie Scott, *School Library Media Centers: Selected Results from the Education Longitudinal Study of 2002 (ELS.-2002 (LACES* 2005-302). U.S. Department of Education, National Center for Education Statistics, (Washington, DC: Government Printing Office) *http://nces.ed.gov/pubs2005/2005302.pdf* (Accessed October 6, 2006).

11. OCLC, 1-19–1-20.

12 Ibid, 6-6.

13. Dennis Dillon, "Strategic Marketing of Electronic Resources," *The Acquisitions Librarian*, 28 (2002) 133.

Basic Marketing and Promotion Concepts

Eleonora Dubicki

Libraries must embrace marketing and promotion in order to communicate with users regarding library products and services. Users associate libraries with books, but few patrons are aware of, or utilize the electronic resources (e-resources)–e-books, e-journals, and databases–that libraries also provide. With the ubiquity of the Web, most users rely on the electronic information they access over the Internet, whether it comes from authoritative sources or not. In order to ensure the continued success of libraries in meeting the evolving needs of our users, libraries must focus concerted efforts on marketing and promoting our eresources –educating our users and potential users on what libraries have to offer.

MARKETING DEFINED

Over the years there have been several adjustments to the definition of marketing. In 2004, the American Marketing Association (AMA) released a revised definition to reflect current practices: "Marketing is an organizational function and a set of processes for creating, communicating and delivering value to customers and for managing customer relationships in ways that benefit the organization and its stakeholders."[1]

In response to the AMA's new definition of marketing, several top marketers have commented on the changes that marketing has undergone in recent years. According to Philip Kotler, "Marketing has moved from a focus on the mass market to a focus on market segments to a focus on one-to-one customer relations."[2] Diane Primo agrees with Kotler that current marketing is focused on building a strategic relationship with the customer, "the goal being to bond that customer . . . to your brand."[3] Libraries can take advantage of this marketing trend in bonding with their customers. Library users have traditionally been very supportive of their libraries, but they also need to support the new eresources that libraries offer in addition to the print materials which they are accustomed to using.

A popular framework for the marketing process is the marketing mix– product, price, place, and promotion, also known as the 4Ps. Marketing requires a critical analysis of the 4Ps to identify benefits and values that a service provides to the customer. Each component of the marketing mix represents a major input into market planning activities:

- Product–actual goods, programs, or services and how they relate to users' needs and wants.
- Price–cost of a product, or cost in terms of time, convenience, and ease of use.
- Place–channels for distributing a product to customers.
- Promotion–various techniques for communicating the features and benefits of a service to users, such as advertising, public relations, incentives, and personal selling.

While the 4Ps are primarily a seller's model used by businesses, libraries can adapt this marketing approach to fit the non-profit library environment. The product in this case is providing information services to our patrons–e-resources. The price component of the marketing mix can be defined by libraries in terms of the convenience and the ease of use our patrons' experience when using e-resources. The place or channel that libraries have for delivering e-resources is online access via the library's Web site, either from the physical library, or remotely from home, office, or school.

WHO DOES THE MARKETING?

According to a 2003 American Library Association (ALA) survey,[4] marketing activities are primarily initiated by library directors. Almost 69 percent of personnel involved with marketing and public relations activities do not have this in their job description. While most librarians have no training in marketing, there clearly is a need for staff with skills in the areas of marketing and promotion. This is supported by the growing number of positions posted for outreach librarians, marketing librarians, public relations and communication officers, which include requirements for core competencies in marketing and promotional skills.

One individual cannot be solely responsible for all of the library's marketing activities; the success of any marketing program relies heavily on involvement and commitment from the entire library staff. Dennis Dillon suggests that "The most effective approach to marketing electronic resources is to involve the entire organization in a strategic program focused on becoming a 'marketing aware' organization."[5] In smaller libraries, the marketing efforts may be led by one person or a small marketing team, but they depend on all staff members, especially those in public services roles, for ongoing assistance in serving customers and carrying out the marketing activities. Libraries with multiple branches, serving a large customer base, are likely to set up a marketing team with representatives from different locations and departments to create a broader base for soliciting input on customer needs. The composition of these multi-person teams also facilitates the implementation of the marketing and promotional campaigns across all branches.

Developing a marketing program may seem to be a daunting task for anyone who has not been trained in marketing. However, there are a number of excellent textbooks and workbooks available on general marketing principles, as well as a number of recently published materials specifically addressing marketing for the library profession. During the last few years, ALA has acknowledged the importance of marketing, and has developed several new programs to advance marketing efforts among libraries. The "@ your Library" campaign has been implemented by all types of libraries across the United States. In addition, the Association for College and Research Libraries (ACRL) has developed a step-by-step guide to developing a marketing plan and creating a promotional campaign, with worksheets to assist in analyzing markets, in its *Strategic Marketing for Academic and Research Libraries Manual.*[6] Similarly, Patricia Fisher and Marseille Pride have published *Blueprint for Your Library Marketing Plan,*[7] which has worksheets and a template for their 12-component marketing plan. *Marketing and Public Relations Practices in College Libraries,*[8] edited by Anita Lindsay, highlights the results of an ALA survey of academic librarians regarding their marketing practices and includes specific examples of marketing and public relations documents from surveyed libraries. Another informational text is Suzanne Walters' *Library Marketing that Works!*[9] which includes sections on developing strategic plans and marketing plans for libraries and explores how technology will drive innovations in marketing.

Hands-on workshops led by marketing specialists are frequently offered as pre-conferences during ALA, ACRL and Public Libraries Association (PLA) conferences. Attendees are able to work through the various components of a marketing plan with the support of the session leader and other librarians. By attending workshops and reading through texts like this one, librarians further develop their marketing skills and can learn from, and build upon, examples of successful marketing programs implemented in other libraries.

MARKETING PLAN

The development of a marketing plan is a good first step in defining what you wish to accomplish, and serves as a guideline for promoting e-resources. The purpose of the marketing plan is to create an organized, manageable plan that incorporates input from library staff and users and also highlights library programs and services to patrons. Unfortunately, only 4.1 percent of small and midsized academic libraries report having a marketing plan.[10] Fisher and Pride contend that "developing and following a well-constructed marketing plan enables your library to come out ahead in the competition–not just to survive, but to thrive."[11]

A marketing plan can also be a valuable tool in securing funding to cover promotional costs. While limited marketing expertise among library staff hampers marketing efforts in many libraries, efforts are further constrained by the lack of funds dedicated for marketing and promotional campaigns–47.3 percent of libraries have no money allocated for marketing, and most use internal resources to produce promotional materials.[12] As a result, costs associated with implementing the marketing plan are often reallocated from already-tight library budgets, or require that outside funding be sought in the form of grants or partnerships. The detailed information gathered for the marketing plan can serve as the basis for requesting those funds.

There are a number of components that are included in a marketing plan, the most important being a project description, definition of marketing goals and objectives, and assessment measures. The plan can be comprised of a couple of pages outlining these components, or it can be expanded to include a thorough analysis of the current library situation and a projection for future positioning. Marketing plan components include:

- Project description–A detailed explanation of the product/service which the library wants to offer or promote.
- Current market–How is the product currently being used and by whom, and who are the library's competitors in providing similar services.
- SWOT analysis–Identification of strengths, weaknesses, opportunities, and threats the library faces with the service.
- Target market–Identification of key user groups for the service based on similar customer needs.
- Marketing goals and objectives–Goals are statements of purpose, such as increasing awareness and usage, and objectives are the measurable means that are used to achieve those goals.
- Marketing strategies–The marketing approach to be used to achieve goals and objectives–selecting the appropriate marketing mix.
- Action plans–Definition of specific steps taken to achieve objectives, identification of costs associated with tasks, a definition of timelines, and the assignment of responsibilities for completion of tasks.

- Evaluation/Assessment techniques–Means for measuring the success or failure of the marketing process.

Marketing plans usually reflect short-term strategies and are revised on an annual basis to reflect changes in the library environment and the revision of goals based on the previous year's experience.

UNDERSTANDING LIBRARY USERS

Since librarians provide personalized service during reference interactions and instructional classes, we have the benefit of understanding many of our users' needs. As a result, we are uniquely tuned-in to the services our patrons will be responsive to, as well as to strategies for communicating with these users effectively. We need to take advantage of our understanding of patron behavior and use it to improve our marketing strategies. If we are still not sure what our customers need, we can conduct market research. Focus groups, interviews or surveys can be used to further investigate customer needs.

Who is the target for your service? Will the service be utilized by all of the library's patrons, or just a smaller segment of users? All library patrons do not have identical needs. Market segmentation is a process to divide the overall market into smaller, homogeneous groups with similar characteristics and needs. In order to market the library's e-resources, it is essential to identify the key market segments likely to make use of e-resources and then to look at methods to satisfy the specific wants and needs of those segments. Promotional campaigns that are tailored to market segments that will use the specific service being promoted are more effective then mass marketing to all library users, many of whom will not use the service. Target marketing allows you to focus efforts on a group that is likely to be receptive to your message–similar to one-on-one marketing. It also makes it easier to communicate with the target group via channels they are familiar with.

In a public library, market segments may be defined by demographics, especially by age, or by psychographics such as lifestyle or hobbies. In an academic library, one type of segmentation might be by academic major, another could be undergraduate, graduate, and doctoral students, and faculty and research groups.

Another aspect of understanding library customers is how the market segments adopt innovations. "Each of these segments will adapt to innovation at different rates and have different comfort levels with the library's use of new or traditional technologies."[13] While current users of e-resources are likely to be among the segments most receptive to new technologies, others may take a wait-and-see approach to trying new services. Levels of comfort with technology may vary among different generations of patrons, and this is another factor that needs to be considered in developing marketing strategies and the appropriate message for each market segment.

CREATING THE MESSAGE

Once a target segment has been identified for promotions, a message must be created that effectively communicates with the intended user segment. The promotional message is used to position the library service and establish the brand–in this case, a specific e-resource.

Promotional materials need to contain a concise, simple message on the benefits which library products can provide. The key in promoting a product is to create a demand and to compel the patron into action to use the product. By targeting a specific market segment, the promotional message can focus on the relevance of a resource to that particular segment. Messages need to be both informative and persuasive. Patrons must be convinced to utilize a product because it will be beneficial to them. Messages also need to capture the patron's attention–graphics grab the reader's attention better than text, and slogans or catchy phrases are even more memorable.

SPREADING THE WORD

Once a message for promoting a product is created, a promotional campaign is developed. It is impossible to promote every library service concurrently, so it is important to clearly define the specific objectives of the promotional campaign. Who is the intended target for the promotion? When will you promote the service? Successful campaigns are not a one-shot deal–repetition is the key to successful promotion.

Where and how will your message reach your patrons? Promotion is a combination of public relations (often free publicity) and marketing activities which will have a cost associated with them. Market plans need to identify the promotional techniques best suited to the service, as well as the needs and preferences of the target audience in the media they are most likely to use. Not all patrons can be reached with one promotional technique. By using a multi-pronged approach with a consistent theme, libraries can more effectively reach their target audience. Not everyone acquires information in the same manner, so multiple approaches for delivering the message are advisable. Some users respond to print promotion, others prefer word-of-mouth communication or online messages. Several vehicles for communicating can be utilized simultaneously, but the message conveyed by each method needs to be consistent as perceived by users:

- Direct selling–Word-of-mouth or personal selling is an extremely powerful promotional tool. Utilize library staff and key faculty members or community leaders as proponents of the library's services. These free media can be very effective if influential, trusted patrons advocate using the library's resources and spread the word to other customers.
- Print brochures–These traditional materials can be available in the library, or they can be mailed to patrons, distributed through the campus bookstore, or placed wherever your patrons are likely to visit.
- Posters–Another traditional promotional technique, posters can be placed wherever your clients will see them, producing a high visual impact. Highlight library patrons on the posters to draw more attention.
- Giveaways–Emblazon your library logo and Web site on items which you can distribute to patrons, such as: pens, pencils, bookmarks, postcards, calendars, tote bags, post-its, coffee mugs, water bottles, business cards, mouse pads, decals, magnets, and key chains.
- Open house–Schedule an open house several times a year to introduce your library staff to patrons and offer demonstrations of the library's e-resources.
- Workshops–Provide training on new services, or create a regular schedule of training sessions for patrons on various e-resources.
- Library catalog–Include links to e-resources directly from the OPAC.
- Research guides/webliographies–Create topic-specific aids with links to reliable and current resources.
- Newsletters–Distribute newsletters in multiple formats depending on the intended target–print, electronic, and web-based. Incorporate brief descriptions of e-resources, highlight subject coverage, offer search tips, and announce training sessions.
- Web site–Library Web pages have a high visual impact on users, are interactive, and can provide direct links to services. Web pages can be used for: new databases announcements with brief descrip-

tions and direct links, "top five" lists with links, or subject-specific lists. Use a "New @ your library" column to keep your patrons current with services. Have links to your library placed in other libraries or community Web sites to draw more users. Or, create a library blog where users can interact with the library.

- Targeted e-mail–Send e-mail to those patrons who will be most interested in a service and will see it as a beneficial product. This is the most personalized marketing technique–directed to a specific market segment. Since everyone is inundated with e-mail, make it worth the recipients' time to read messages from their library.
- RSS feeds–Allow patrons to sign up for automatic notification of news items from the library.
- Course management systems–Include links to library resources in courseware such as Blackboard, WebCT, and Desire2Learn to augment course materials. Faculty can facilitate student connections to generic or course-specific resources, including reading assignments, tutorials, or e-resources, as well as online reference assistance in completing research.
- Advertising–Exploit media outlets for the community or college campus such as local/school newspapers and cable television programs to promote library services.

Prior to implementing a promotional campaign, it is essential to keep library staff fully informed on which services will be promoted and to provide sufficient training on using the services. Staff need to be totally comfortable with accessing and completing searches with the e-resources being promoted. By training the trainer, you build confidence and gain strong advocates for the service, and the campaign becomes a more cohesive effort with the participation of all library staff.

EVALUATION

Evaluations of the marketing plan process should be ongoing, not just at the end of the campaign. By regularly reviewing the goals and objectives in the plan, adjustments or revisions can be made, or a complete restructuring of certain elements of the process can be incorporated if necessary. Feedback on the effectiveness of the promotional campaign can be gathered from measurable objectives or direct comments from patrons. Marketing is always dynamic because customer needs and library services change, perhaps necessitating modifications to the marketing plan.

When the library undertakes a new e-resources promotional campaign, it is important to assess the success of the stated goals, to ensure promotions are reaching the intended audience, and resulting in increased awareness and usage of services. Analyzing pre- and post-campaign e-resources usage statistics is a basic measure of effectiveness and will indicate whether patrons have been successfully enticed to use the service. Library advisory groups can also serve as a litmus test for effectiveness of promotional efforts. The benefit of talking to a group of users is the specific feedback they can provide on what worked in the campaign. Usage statistics can quantify actual changes in usage, but advisory or focus groups can provide better data on why a campaign was successful. This feedback can help the library determine whether the promotions were successful and what modifications should be incorporated into subsequent promotions.

CONCLUSION

Marketing and promotion play a key role in assuring the viability of libraries in this era of rapidly-changing technological advances. The promotion of e-resources exemplifies how the library is adapting to user needs for convenient access to electronic information available anytime and from anyplace. In effect, we are promoting how services offered by the library extend beyond the physical building to provide our patrons with high-quality information in the manner by which they wish to access it. Libraries need to create a buzz among their users about all these new e-resources, and continue to strengthen relationships with patrons by providing high-value service.

While this chapter serves to introduce the reader to the fundamental concepts of marketing and promotion, the other chapters in the book provide details of marketing and promotional techniques which have been used by public, special and academic libraries. Many of the techniques included in this chapter have been implemented by the libraries, and their experiences can serve as models for developing your own marketing program.

NOTES

1. Lisa M. Keefe, "What is the meaning of 'Marketing'?" *Marketing News*, 38, no. 5 (September 15, 2004):17.

2. Philip Kotler, "Marketing Redefined Nine Top Marketers offer their Personal Definitions," *Marketing News* 38, no. 5 (September 15, 2004): 16.

3. Diane Primo, "Marketing Redefined Nine Top Marketers offer their Personal Definitions," *Marketing News*, 38, no. 5 (September 15, 2004): 16.

4. Anita Rothwell Lindsay, *Marketing and Public Relations Practices in College Libraries* (Chicago: American Library Association, 2004).

5. Dennis Dillon, "Strategic Marketing of Electronic Resources," *The Acquisitions Librarian* 28 (2002): 117.

6. ACRL Association of College and Research Libraries, *Strategic Marketing for Academic and Research Libraries Participant Manual* (2003). http://www.ala.org/ala/acrl/acrlissues/marketingyourlib/ParticipantManual.doc (accessed October 6, 2006)

7. Patricia Fisher and Marseille M. Pride, *Blueprint for Your Library Marketing Plan* (Chicago: American Library Association, 2006).

8. Lindsay.

9. Suzanne Walters, *Library Marketing That Works!* (New York: Neal Schuman Publishers, Inc., 2004).

10. Lindsay, 5.

11. Fisher, vii.

12. Lindsay, 8.

13. Dillon, 131.

Thinking Outside of the Library Box: The Library Communication Manager

Monica Metz-Wiseman
Skye L. Rodgers

Technology has brought radical changes to the academic library world. Historically, libraries and librarians functioned as intermediaries in the search for information. Today, Google and other search engines have dramatically changed the information landscape. For the first time, libraries face the reality of competition. Phrases and acronyms such as "business models," "market share," and "ROI" are being used to describe library operations. The transformed academic library represents a significant philosophical shift from the days when libraries and librarians held a virtual monopoly as the gatekeepers of information. This transformation is being driven largely by rapidly and continuously changing technology which, in turn, is creating new generations of learners who seek information in ways increasingly different from the past.

The University of South Florida's (USF) Library System consists of four campus libraries, a special library, and a medical library. The USF Libraries provide access to more than two million volumes and an extensive collection of electronic resources (e-resources) with 54,000 ebooks, 150,000 digital images, 6,500 e-journal subscriptions, and 500 databases that supply another 13,000 unique e-journal titles. For more than a decade, the USF Libraries have engaged in the marketing of e-resources. As a multi-campus university with over 43,000 students, this marketing effort took several forms from its early initiatives to the present. This chapter will present the stages of this marketing program as it moved from a team-based approach to a centralized function within the Libraries administered by a Communication Manager. It will evaluate each approach and address why marketing was an early concern of the USF Libraries.

THE VIRTUAL LIBRARY PROJECT

In 1995, a comprehensive effort was underway to deliver as much content and as many services beyond the walls of the USF Libraries as was possible. Recognizing the revolution occurring in scholarly communication, the USF Libraries sought a comprehensive approach to planning, organizing, and implementing this initiative, known as the USF Libraries Virtual Library Project. A document entitled "The USF

Libraries Virtual Library Project: A Blueprint for Development" served as a guide for the project.[1] The Virtual Library Project began with the creation of eight project teams: Electronic Collections Team, Digitization Project Group, Electronic Journal Project Group, Metadata Project Group, Electronic Reserves/ILL Project Group, Staff Development/Instruction Team, Virtual Library Implementation Team, and Interface Design Project Group. Early in the process, two teams merged (Electronic Collections and Electronic Journal Project Group), and new teams were created as the "product," the Virtual Library Project, began to emerge. The second wave of teams under the umbrella of the Virtual Library Project included the Electronic Theses and Dissertations Team, Marketing Team, Outcomes Assessment, and Statistics.

Marketing and planning were central to the success of the Virtual Library Project. Marketing in this context was defined by Kotler. "Marketing is the analysis, planning, implementation, and control of carefully formulated programs designed to bring about voluntary exchanges of values with target audiences for the purposes of achieving organizational objectives. It relies heavily on designing the organization's offerings in terms of the target market's needs and desires, and on using effective pricing, communication, and distribution to inform, motivate, and service the markets."[2]

Weingand summarized seven points to this approach:

1. Marketing is a managerial process involving analysis, planning, implementation, and control.
2. Marketing is concerned with carefully formulated programs – not random actions–designed to achieve desired response.
3. Marketing seeks to bring about voluntary exchanges.
4. Marketing selects target markets and does not seek to be all things to all people.
5. Marketing is directly correlated to the achievement of organizational objectives.
6. Marketing places emphasis on the target market's (consumer's) needs and desires rather than on the producer's preferences.
7. Marketing utilizes what has been termed the "marketing mix," or the four Ps–product, pricing, place/distribution and promotion/communication–with the expansion to the six Ps with the addition of prelude (the marketing audit) and postlude (the evaluation).[3]

The Virtual Library Project was based on comprehensive planning and analysis involving the user community and the library staff. This process included a comprehensive literature review, attendance at relevant conferences, the convening of thirteen specific focus groups based on user populations, and a survey of eight peer institutions. The focus groups confirmed the need for quick, intuitive online delivery of content and services. As one participant said, "a virtual library should make my life easier."[4] The Virtual Library Project employed a merged marketing and planning process that relied heavily on user needs. The project held to the statement that "marketing without planning is an exercise; planning without marketing is a formality."[5]

The team-based format of the Virtual Library Project represented a significant shift from the more traditional and hierarchical organizational structures that preceded this initiative and relied on three main elements. First, the team approach was an opportunity for librarians and library staff to provide leadership beyond the traditional hierarchy of the USF Libraries. Paraprofessionals, support staff, and librarians shared responsibilities, distributed assignments equally, and became educated on the issues together. For many, this was a rare and unprecedented opportunity for participation of this nature. This flattened organizational structure spurred creativity, productivity, and buy-in. Second, the team-based model mandated the integration of library staff affiliated with technical services and public services. The third element of the Virtual Library team-based model was inclusion of staff from all of the USF Libraries, where practical. For many members of the staff, Virtual Library teams afforded an opportunity to work with library staff from other USF Libraries for the first time. This crossover from geographic divisions spilled over to other library work beyond the immediate team tasks.

Involving more than 100 librarians and support staff from USF's four campuses and special libraries, the Virtual Library Project teams met, deliberated, developed timelines, held planning retreats, and acted on a number of projects such as the creation of a digitization center; online interlibrary loan through the acquisition of ILLiad; the first online e-reserve system among the Florida universities; the migration from print to electronic theses and dissertations; and the rapid movement from print to an electronic-only format for indexes, abstracting services, journals, newspapers, and reference materials.

THE MARKETING TEAM

One of the emerging themes from the planning phase for the Virtual Library Project was the need to create user awareness regarding the availability of e-resources. This was a primary motivation leading to the creation of the Marketing Team. Yet, the need for communicating progress to the USF community on the development of the Virtual Library meant that the Marketing Team was responsible for the marketing not only of e-resources, but also of the Virtual Library Project as a whole. Tasks for the Marketing Team then expanded to include the promotion, communication, and branding of the Virtual Library to encourage recognition and use of the USF Libraries online offerings. Branding included the naming of the USF Virtual Library and the development of a logo (see Figure 1) that was used on posters, publications, postcards, bookmarks, pens and pencils, user aids, the Web site, mouse pads, and even apparel and tote bags.

For five years, the Marketing Team promoted the use of hundreds of online resources and communicated progress on the development of the Virtual Library. The chair of the Marketing Team, with other team

FIGURE 1. Virtual Library art element developed by the Marketing Team.

Used with permission.

members, provided details on these activities in the book chapter, "Marketing the Virtual Library."[6]

The Marketing Team engaged in a wide variety of marketing strategies:

- Launched the Virtual Library with an open house, followed by annual Virtual Library birthdays complete with balloons, cake, and giveaways.
- Hosted wine and cheese receptions for faculty.
- Organized seminars addressing the future of libraries, collections, and services.
- Purchased Virtual Library materials such as pens, pencils, bookmarks, professionally created brochures for distribution at bibliographic instruction sessions, as well as at freshman and new faculty orientations.
- Offered brief presentations at faculty departmental meetings and took any opportunity on campus to promote and communicate developments with the Virtual Library.
- Enlisted the help of instruction and collection development librarians who promoted online resources in the classroom and to faculty.
- Worked with the Electronic Collections Team to solicit help from vendors for product promotion.
- Created a flowchart or template for promoting resources.
- Worked closely with the Interface Design Project Group (responsible for library Web pages) to ensure appropriate "product" placement.
- Worked with the USF Marketing Department's faculty and graduate-level students to develop five distinct marketing plans for the Virtual Library and e-resources that included the identification of: market, product, competitive, distribution and macro situations; strengths and weaknesses; external threats and opportunities; target markets; objectives and marketing strategies; and action plans.

CHALLENGES AND OPPORTUNITIES: WHAT WORKED, WHAT DIDN'T

What Worked

The planning process provided the Marketing Team with a philosophy and a blueprint for their work. The team approach, with a combination of librarians and support staff, allowed for engagement at all levels. The support staff and the librarians understood the importance of organizing an open house and the distribution of marketing materials to six geographically dispersed libraries. Self-selection of the team also predisposed engagement in marketing activities. Each team created a Web site with membership, charge, timeline, and meeting minutes. Progress was easy to gauge.

From no previous concerted marketing efforts on the part of the USF Libraries, there emerged a focused, directed effort derived from a group of dedicated volunteers. As a task and goal-oriented group, they enjoyed early success. Faculty and administrators quickly began to identify the online USF Libraries as the Virtual Library. It appeared in syllabi and course packs. Students were sent to the reference desk by their faculty to "use the Virtual Library."

The success of the marketing efforts could be seen by examining electronic resource usage statistics. Within the Florida university system, use statistics tracked to USF for shared e-resources were consistently at a higher level than universities of similar or larger size. Use statistics for locally held resources saw exponential growth from one year to the next.

An unexpected result of the marketing strategy was the longevity of the Virtual Library "product," which continued to be referred to and appeared on syllabi years after the end of the project.

What Didn't

When the Virtual Library Teams neared their end of their five-year tenures, the intent was to merge Virtual Library Teams within traditional library activities. Similar to the Electronic Collections Team in that there was no equivalent within the traditional library, the Marketing Team was one of the first to disperse whereas the Electronic Collections Team continued until 2004. Most of the members stayed on the Marketing Team for the duration of its existence, but recruiting new members was difficult, particularly since participation on any of the Virtual Library Teams was voluntary. As Weingand states, libraries "have been confident that their product had such intrinsic merit that clients automatically would be attracted, or in a more moralistic vein, believed that people 'should' use the library," and this opinion endures among many in the field.[7] While the original team members understood the value of marketing and promotion, that value was not universally held. The task of a focused, intense, continuous marketing program could not be sustained beyond five years with a dedicated group of volunteers. Team members dropped off the Marketing Team citing time constraints.

Furthermore, it was sometimes difficult to accommodate the local interests, goals, and missions of all of the USF Libraries. There were significant differences in budgets, populations served, collections, and staffing that brought challenges to this process. Given the number of Virtual Library Teams, not every USF Library could afford to continue to have a representative on the Marketing Team.

Marketing focused exclusively on online resources and services. There was no attempt to integrate these resources into the physical libraries with print, microform, and multimedia collections.

Next Phase: The USF Libraries Marketing Committee

In 1998, USF was named a "Research I" university by the Florida Board of Regents and since 2000 was listed in the top rank of research universities by the Carnegie Foundation for the Advancement of Learning. To address the changing circumstances, the Library and Information Science Task Force was formed. This was a university-level task force formed to recommend strategies that would assist the libraries in adapting to the university's new mandate as a Research I university.

These events had a profound effect on the USF Library System. Until this time, the main campus libraries had served the needs of the undergraduate and graduate populations as equitably as possible, at the expense of building collections of distinction. The radical changes in university mission and system organization, the fairly sudden and dramatic proliferation of online resources, and technological advancements coupled with a period of little or no funding increases created a very dynamic, volatile environment for the library operations.

It was decided during this time to integrate the activities of the Virtual Library Project into the folds of the existing workflows and departments of the USF Libraries. The Marketing Team officially disbanded in the fall of 2000 with a series of recommendations for the directors to ensure the continuity of this work.

In its place emerged a new Marketing Committee charged with responsibilities for providing leadership in marketing library resources and services, both for the physical library and the Virtual Library. The committee, which included the Vice President of USF Media Relations as well as representatives from all the libraries, was charged to develop a marketing plan focusing on the creative and content aspects of marketing the USF Libraries. The group met from April through June of 2001. The plan resulting from their efforts outlined why a marketing plan was important, the goals and objectives of the plan, and identified targeted group characteristics.[8] In keeping with the recommendation from the Virtual Library Implementation Team, implementation was left largely to a newly hired "Coordinator of Information and Publications." However, even though the Marketing Plan was written and a specialist hired, the plan was never fully implemented as there was no transition from one plan to the next and the focus on the marketing of e-resources shifted.

The hiring of the Coordinator of Information and Publications had recently come about as a result of exposure to the graphic arts abilities of a temporary employee. Recognizing the possibilities with regards to the production of more professional flyers and brochures, the dean began looking for a permanent employee with similar qualifications. The resulting hire had a journalism background as opposed to graphic arts; however, in addition to assisting with the Marketing Plan, this person began the process of introducing formalized, comprehensive marketing strategies to the Libraries. During the employee's tenure, from 2000 through 2002, marketing project accomplishments included:

- development of formal display procedures for all library displays
- introduction of lecture series featuring special guest speakers from USF, the community, or other academic libraries
- use of offsite graphics and printing companies to produce library promotional materials
- development of the USF Libraries logo (see Figure 2) for branding purposes

These activities helped show the USF community and USF Media Relations that the Libraries had many interesting and newsworthy projects and accomplishments–enough to finally warrant the attention of University Media Relations and inclusion in university publications.

During this period, the marketing of e-resources had reached a plateau. Announcements of new online resources continued to be sent out via email to the university community; lists of new online resources were created and distributed; presentations were made at faculty meetings; an annual meeting was held to update faculty on collections; reference librarians continued to promote the use of online resources through chat, email, at the reference desk, and in the classroom; and the library promoted access to its online offerings through Blackboard, a course management system.

FIGURE 2. Current Library System art element initially developed by the Coordinator of Information and Publication and subsequently modified by the current Communication Manager.

Used with permission.

CHALLENGES AND OPPORTUNITIES:
WHAT WORKED, WHAT DIDN'T

What Worked

During this phase, the USF Libraries were able to develop a comprehensive marketing plan for the libraries that integrated all facets of their operations and introduced the concept of providing specific target audiences with the information that they required as opposed to pushing specific products to every audience at once. The hiring of a specialist allowed someone with more education and work experience in marketing to implement the Marketing Plan while gaining important insight from the larger committee.

What Didn't

While the Marketing Plan was an important step in the right direction, it fell short of being complete. While the objectives, target audiences, and library staff responsibilities toward the marketing effort were well thought out and clearly stated, there were no accompanying strategies, timelines, or specific evaluation techniques attached. The Marketing Committee disbanded once the Marketing Plan had been developed leaving full implementation to a newly hired individual, along with a high level of independence.

In the absence of clear objectives and strategies, the USF Libraries sought marketing experience exclusively in the Coordinator position, rather than marketing and public relations experience. The Coordinator position also had difficulties in the reporting structure. Initially the coordinator reported to the Director of Development, thus subsuming the marketing function under the development function. This resulted in many of the Libraries' efforts in other areas being overlooked. Subsequently, the Coordinator began reporting directly to the dean, which allowed for a more holistic approach to marketing.

PHASE 3: HIRING A COMMUNICATION MANAGER

During the same time period, from 2000 to 2002, the Dean of the Library System was approached by the University's School of Mass Communication, which was interested in conducting a research study to determine the requirements for an academic library seeking "premier" research status as defined by the organization that sets standards for such facilities–the Association of Research Libraries. This collaboration began an intensive and thorough education of the Libraries' administrators regarding marketing, public relations, and what these functions could accomplish in an academic library setting. The study was undertaken by public relations professor, Barbara Petersen and her students and resulted in the submission of the report, "Communication Management in an Academic Library Setting."[9]

Because of the necessity to limit the project scope, the final research report focused primarily on the relationship between academic librarians and research faculty. However, the report included a strong recommendation to establish a managerial communication function within the Libraries: "Appoint a management level employee who will be in charge of internal and external communication for the Tampa Campus Library, and who must report directly to the dean of the library system. This managerial employee must fully understand research faculty needs and expectations in order to develop effective strategies to establish relationships with them. The most critical requirement for this manager is that s/he has relevant public relations experience and education in order to create and sustain a dialogue between researchers and librarians."[10]

This recommendation resulted in an overhaul of the previous coordinator position and was implemented in 2003 when a Communication Manager was hired. The new Communication Manager position draws on a study of public relations practitioners that identified the characteristics of "excellence" in an organization's public relations function.[11] As a result, this position now reports directly to the Dean of the Library System and has a high level of autonomy and decision-making authority in planning and implementing communication strategies as recommended in the study. The current Communication Manager holds a Master's degree in Public Relations. Although Grunig's 2002 study does not show that a high-level, discipline-specific education is required for an organization to have an effective public relations function,[12] it could be argued that because public relations is a relatively new function in academic libraries, and specifically at USF, education in public relations is advantageous to allow for the function to develop effectively.

In the marketing and public relations fields, there are several worldviews to which practitioners may subscribe depending on their experience and education. Many organizations consider marketing to be the primary method of communication. Marketing is a function that focuses on promoting products to its end users, while public relations serves to create awareness of the organization's products. This view does not take into account those constituents that are not end users of an organization but have the ability to affect the operation of an organization. Public relations is defined as "the management of communication between an organization and its publics."[13] These publics, or audiences, in an academic library setting can include university administration, employees, government regulators, professional associations, and donors, to name a few.

The shift of the USF Libraries from exclusively a marketing focus to one that integrates both marketing and public relations supports a coordinated, balanced, and strategic approach to communication activities, including both public relations and marketing, supported by research and followed up with evaluation.

The practical implications of employing this coordinated approach means that although marketing is clearly needed to publicize and develop the Libraries' online resources, these marketing efforts become part of a comprehensive strategy that uses segmentation to define target audiences for promotions. By employing segmentation, the organization does not waste resources trying to appeal to a mass audience, and much greater effectiveness is achieved when those most receptive to your message are targeted.

A profile can be created of the organization's most important audiences and used to further research their needs for resources and services employing information gathered during the communication audit. This information also allows for the prioritization of audiences. For example, segmentation in preparation for marketing an e-resource will allow for the identification of the most effective communication channels to the students and faculty who would find the resource of the most value or interest. Segmentation will also allow for the appending of messages that support the use of the resource, such as instruction or tutorial information, the availability of email alerts, or the listing of specific topics.

Once target audiences are identified, profiled, and prioritized, a custom communication plan is created. The plan ensures all relevant information has been taken into account, the time and resources necessary are available, a timeline is established, and evaluation techniques from which to measure the plan's effectiveness are incorporated. Such a plan is very important for new public relations and marketing areas because it helps to build an information repository that will assist in developing the responsibilities, personnel, and fiscal resources for the area. All plans should include the following procedures:

- Identify effective and efficient communication channels for each public. Be sure to incorporate interactivity and feedback mechanisms.
- Create messages that are written for the specific public, ensure the messages are relevant to that public, and the appropriate communication channels are used to reach the audience.
- Assign resources (labor, money) according to priority.
- Develop evaluation techniques.

The use of the approach outlined above has resulted in the integration of most of the Library System communication efforts. This has allowed the Library System to focus on strategic priorities and utilize communication channels in a coordinated manner that benefits and encourages the increasing integration of resources, both electronic and print, and the targeted services that support their use. New initiatives that have directly benefited the marketing of e-resources include:

- A new faculty newsletter (see Figures 3 and 4) containing descriptions of all new e-resources, produced as a print and online publication that is distributed at the beginning of each semester.

- The development of a staff newsletter (see Figure 5) to inform staff in all the university libraries of new e-resources, delivered as an email publication every two weeks during the school year.
- A "News" section on the USF Libraries Web site which is updated to promote newly acquired e-resources as well as databases on a trial basis, and encourages feedback from patrons.
- A projection screen in the Tampa Library's Information Commons that markets new e-resources on a continuous-loop basis.
- An LED sign installed in the first floor lobby of the Tampa Library that advertises new e-resources on an 8-second loop, as well as a lobby display space to promote e-resources
- Printed graphic materials (see Figures 6 and 7) promoting e-resources created and disseminated on an as-needed basis.
- The development of a new USF Libraries Web site (see Figure 8), created under the direction of the Communication Manager. The Web site will support easier access to e-resources and will be fully integrated with support from librarians, help pages, and tutorials. The content management system for the Web site will also allow for the librarians most closely involved with the e-resources to communicate and market directly to interested audiences.

All of the initiatives listed above directly benefit the marketing of e-resources, yet none are limited to the marketing of electronic materials. The channels are also used to disseminate other important messages to the targeted groups. This allows for optimal management of available resources.

CHALLENGES AND OPPORTUNITIES: WHAT WORKS, WHAT WE'RE WORKING ON

What Works

The research conducted by Dr. Barbara Petersen and her students represented the first attempt to examine the USF Libraries and their situation from a public relations point of view. This resulted in a fresh and unique vantage point from which the library administration could examine both their history and their future. The collaboration required during the research process resulted in a "Hawthorne Effect" (that is, just by doing the research, there is an effect on the research subjects and those conducting the research) that educated and informed all participants as to the discipline of public relations and the benefits that public relations strategies could have on library operations.

FIGURE 3. Electronic Resources are featured in *Library Leads*, a newsletter distributed each semester to faculty and researchers on all USF campuses.

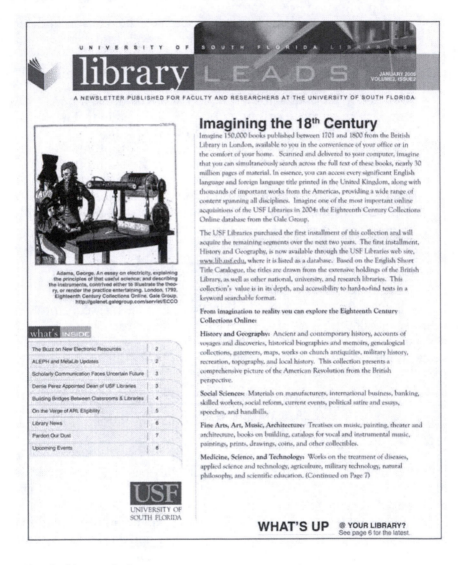

Used with permission.

FIGURE 4. Every issue of *Library Leads* contains a brief description of newly acquired electronic resources.

The Buzz on New Electronic Resources

DOES HEAVY TRAFFIC ON DEAD-END SEARCH ENGINES GET YOU DOWN?

ARE YOU STUCK IN A RESEARCH RUSH HOUR IN YOUR QUEST TO COMPLETE THAT ARTICLE FOR PUBLICATION OR CONFERENCE PAPER?

DON'T PANIC! HELP IS ON THE WAY IN THE FORM OF SOME RECENTLY ACQUIRED ELECTRONIC RESOURCES NOW AVAILABLE THROUGH THE USF LIBRARIES WEBSITE. WE ENCOURAGE YOU TO KICK THE "DIGITAL" TIRES AND GIVE THESE NEW ACADEMIC RESOURCES A TEST DRIVE.

See descriptions of selected resources below. For a complete list of resources acquired this year see www.lib.usf.edu.

If you ever require immediate roadside assistance while stopped along the information research superhighway, please contact a reference librarian in the USF Library System!

Elsevier Science Direct E-Journal Backfiles: Business, Management, and Accounting
This journal backfile collection provides online access to 59 journals in business, management, and accounting beginning with the first volume published. The oldest title dates back to 1960. It includes top titles such as European Management Journal, Journal of Management, Organizational Dynamics, Long Range Planning and Accounting, and Organizations and Society. It is fully integrated with the current titles in this area along with related journals in the Elsevier ScienceDirect online journal collection.

Royal Society of Chemistry Journals and Archive
Includes seventeen significant chemistry journals such as Chemical Communications, Faraday Discussions, and Dalton Transactions. USF also subscribes to the RSC archive allowing access to the full text of more than 200,000 published articles from 1841 to 1996.

RIA Checkpont
Provides authoritative tax and accounting information. You can search from a number of practice areas or browse through Checkpoint's contents using the Table of Contents feature in the same way you would scan the headings in a book's table of contents for items of use to you.
USF subscribes to:
• RIA Academic Advantage Library;
• Tax Advisors Planning System;
• Pen & Ben Essentials on Checkpoint; and
• GAAP Compliance.

Blackwell Synergy Humanities and Social Sciences (HSS) Collection
In 2003, USF held 132 print titles within this collection. By acquiring the entire HSS collection in 2004 and providing online access, we added 218 important journals in the humanities and social sciences for a total of 350 scholarly titles. Along with the STM (Sciences, Technology, Medicine) collection, Blackwell Synergy is comprised of 670 journal titles, many published for scholarly and professional societies. Access to the HSS collection includes all available online files dateing back to volume one for 50 journals. Synergy also features Online Early articles, which are posted online before the print issue is published. Online Early is available for many key titles.

Encyclopedia of Library and Information Science (online)
The online Encyclopedia of Library and Information Science is the second edition, revised and expanded, and published in May of 2003. Targets new movements in the distribution, acquisition, and development of print and online media—addressing recruitment, information management, advances in digital technology and encoding, intellectual property issues, and hardware, software, and database selection and design.

Encyclopedia of Public Administration and Public Policy (online)
The Encyclopedia of Public Administration and Public Policy was published in May of 2003 and edited by Jack Rabin, editor of the International Journal of Public Administration. This online encyclopedia covers current topics such as federalism in Homeland Security and crisis management. Includes policy decisions and fields such as privatization, biomedical ethics, education, diversity, and judicial ethics; decisions and policies, spanning the Nuremberg trials to the Civil Service Reform Act of 1978; and current administrative practices and models with articles such as "Electronic Government," and "Economic Theories of Administration."

Journals@OVID: Lippincott Williams & Wilkins
Funded by the USF Shimberg Health Sciences Library, on behalf of all the USF Libraries this collection of over 200 online journals combines essential core titles in nutrition, nursing, bioscience, aging studies, oncology, sports medicine, with specialized titles in the areas of infectious diseases, cardiology, and more. Includes titles such as AIDS, Annals of Surgery, the Clinical Journal of Sports Medicine, and Nursing Research. This collection is incorporated in the Journal@OVID collection.

2 UNIVERSITY OF SOUTH FLORIDA LIBRARIES

Used with permission.

FIGURE 5. New e-resources are highlighted in *Off the Shelf*, the Library System's bi-monthly e-newsletter.

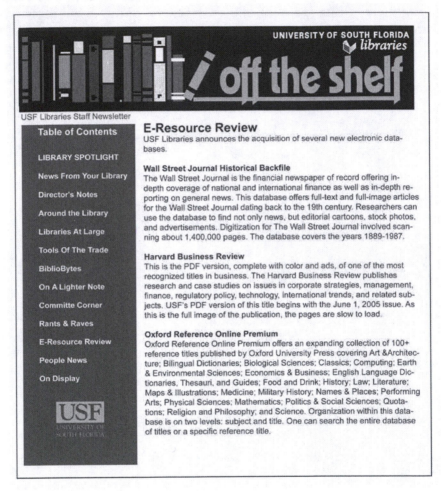

Used with permission.

The research project recommendation to hire a Communication Manager resulted in a position description with well-defined goals. This in turn led to the hiring of a candidate with the appropriate education, experience, and expertise to be successful in the position in terms of quality and effectiveness. The new Communication Manager developed a workable, comprehensive, and strategic planning system that encom-

FIGURE 6. Library Communications uses the back of "new book" flags to promote e-resources.

New E-Resource:

Smithsonian Global Sound for Libraries

Produced in partnership with Smithsonian Folkways Recordings, the database presents more than 35,000 individual tracks of music, spoken word, and natural and human-made sounds. The play list includes the published recordings owned by the non-profit Smithsonian Folkways Recordings label and the archival audio collections of the legendary Folkways Records and other labels.

Featured music includes American Folk; Blues; Bluegrass; Old Time Country; American Indian; World; Jazz; Classical & Broadway; Children's; and spoken word and sounds. Listeners can browse through the music any number of ways—they can choose their favorite sounds from a list of categories; or they can browse by artist (Woody Guthrie, Lead Belly, and others); cultural group; country, with more than 150 countries represented; or by instrument.

Soundtracks can be placed in Blackboard, webpages, in emails, and in Word documents although the computer requesting these soundtracks must be connected to the USF network.

Used with permission.

FIGURE 7. This poster for a newly acquired collection accompanied a promotional lobby display.

Used with permission.

passes the entire USF Library System. Instead of one overarching Marketing Committee, the Communication Manager brings groups together for specific projects.

Having a centralized public relations and marketing function allowed other staff members to focus on priorities in their areas while still being involved in projects on an as-needed basis.

What We're Working On

Centralizing the marketing function has resulted in a greater separation of the marketing and public relations activities from the day-to-day work of most library employees. This can at times result in a communication disconnect, although frequent communication with

FIGURE 8. The newly designed USF Libraries Web site will serve as an easy-to-navigate portal to all e-resources with built-in promotional opportunities.

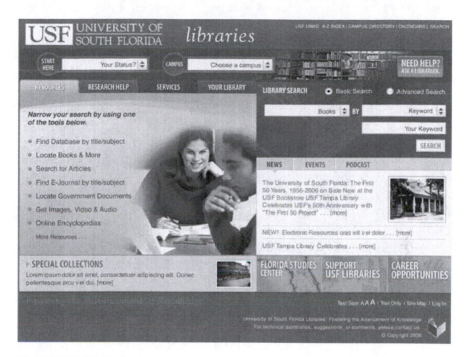

Used with permission.

colleagues is attempted. Staff understanding of the marketing and public relations function is still not complete and misunderstandings of its scope and intent still occur. Although this situation has improved, this area still suffers from a lack of staff understanding as to what public relations is and what it can accomplish in an organization. More education is needed.

Even though the communication area has been able to expand both in terms of staffing and fiscal resources, the area still suffers from inadequate resources. The result is that areas of library services and materials are not being adequately represented in public relations and marketing efforts. Since the formalization of the new communication area is still quite new, it is hoped that with the further establishment of public relations and marketing infrastructure, this situation will improve.

CONCLUSIONS

In the past decade, academic libraries have faced many challenges, and the USF Libraries are no exception. It is precisely in this type of environment that researchers find organizations are most in need of public relations support. Spicer noted that "Politics most often occur when the organization faces uncertainty, when there is conflict, and when decision making is not routine . . . these are the very organizational conditions that bring about the need for public relations."[14] Even without a tradition of employing marketing and public relations in their organization, the USF Libraries recognized a need and attempted to fulfill that need. This is a trend being seen across the country, and the experiences of the USF Libraries are not unique.

In 2006, the authors conducted an unpublished, online survey of academic libraries regarding public relations and marketing personnel. Just over half of the 129 respondents indicated they employ full- or part-time staff members to handle publicity, public relations, media relations, event planning, marketing, or other communication-related duties. Over three-quarters of respondents also indicated a medium-to-high priority for the next staff member hired to have public relations and marketing experience. Almost ninety percent of these respondents said that their top communicator had a medium-to-high level of decision-making authority with 49 out of 70 stating that their top communicator reported directly to the Dean, University Librarian, or Director of the Library. This contrasts with previous surveys of this type. In 1979, a survey by the Association of Research Libraries on external communication, did not ask any of these questions, assuming that all communications were performed in conjunction with the campus public relations and marketing functions.[15] A 1999 study showed much improvement in this area and indicated that over half the libraries that reported had some type of public relations function.[16] The American Library Association published a survey in 2004 as part of the Clip Note series which also showed an increase in public relations and marketing awareness and activities by college and university libraries with over 92% of respondents indicating these activities were important or very important to fulfilling their mission.[17] However, this awareness was not shown to be translated into assigning time and financial resources to this effort with 81.8% of respondent libraries allocating only five hours or less and 71.5% allocating less than $500 to marketing and public relations activities.[18]

While the road over the past decade has had its ups and downs, the experience of the USF Libraries may have implications for other academic libraries going through similar circumstances:

- The academic library today has competition and will need to continue communicating its relevance in order to maintain and expand its position in the center of university life.
- Administrators and employees of libraries need to be educated regarding marketing and public relations in order to effectively take advantage of what these functions have to offer.
- Public relations and marketing work most effectively when integrated in a coordinated, balanced and strategic plan.

The efforts undertaken at the University of South Florida Libraries to promote awareness and use of rapidly expanding collections of e-resources have taken several forms over the past decade: the team approach of bringing together people from each library to develop marketing strategies, the committee approach of creating a strategic marketing plan, and finally, the hiring of a Communication Manager to centrally coordinate both planning and implementation of marketing and public relations strategies. Each approach has its own benefits and drawbacks and was ultimately essential for the development of an overall understanding of marketing and public relations. However, the current situation for academic libraries requires careful use of time and financial resources. The USF Libraries have found that the best way to manage these resources, specifically its marketing and public relations efforts, is through the use of a centralized function overseen by a communication professional. This approach has somewhat subjugated strategies and tactics focused solely on e-resources in favor of a more holistic model of marketing and public relations for all library services and resources. Ongoing adjustments will be needed to achieve the right balance.

NOTES

1. Monica Metz-Wiseman, Susan Silver, Ardis Hanson, Judy Johnston, Kim Grohs, Tina Neville, Ed Sanchez, and Carolyn Gray. *The USF Libraries Virtual Library Project: A Blueprint for Development.* (Tampa: University of South Florida, 1996).

2. Philip Kotler, *Marketing for Nonprofit Organizations.* (Englewood Cliffs, N.J., Prentice-Hall, 1975), 5.

3. Darlene E. Weingand, *Marketing/Planning Library and Information Services.* (Littleton, Col.: Libraries Unlimited, 1987), 5-6.

4. Metz-Wiseman, *The USF Libraries Virtual Library Project,* 58.

5. Weingand, *Marketing/Planning Library and Information Services,* 17.

6. Kim Grohs, Caroline Reed, and Nancy Allen, "Marketing the Virtual Library" in *Building a Virtual Library,* ed. Ardis Hanson and Bruce L. Levin (Hershey, PA: Information Science Pub, 2003).

7. Weingand, *Marketing/Planning Library and Information Services,* 5.

8. Kathy Arsenault, Nancy Allen, Teresa Brown, Dan Cassedy, Te Leone, and Jim Vastine. *Marketing Plan.* (Tampa: University of South Florida, 2001).

9. Barbara Petersen, et al. *Communication Management in an Academic Library Setting.* Presented to the Communication Sciences Division, Sixth International, Interdisciplinary, Public Relations Research Conference, University of Miami, Miami, March 20-23, 2003.

10. Ibid, 31-32.

11. Larissa A. Grunig, James A. Grunig, and David M. Dozier. *Excellent Public Relations and Effective Organizations: A Study of Communication Management in Three Countries.* (Mahwah, NJ: Lawrence Erlbaum, 2002).

12. Ibid.

13. James E. Grunig and Todd Hunt, *Managing Public Relations.* (Forth Worth: Harcourt Brace Jovanovich, 1984), 6.

14. C. Spicer, "Assumptions" in *Organizational Public Relations: A Political Perspective,* ed. C. Spicer (Mahwah, NJ: Erlbaum, 1997).

15. Association of Research Libraries and Systems and Procedures Exchange Center. *External Communication* (Washington, DC: Association of Research Libraries, Office of Management Studies, 1979).

16. Evelyn C. Smykla, Association of Research Libraries, and Systems and Procedures Exchange Center. *Marketing and Public Relations Activities in ARL Libraries: a SPEC Kit.* (Washington, DC: Association of Research Libraries, Office of Leadership and Management Services, 1999).

17. Anita Rothwell Lindsay, comp. *Marketing and Public Relations Practices in College Libraries* (Chicago: College Library Information Packet Committee, Association of College and Research Libraries, 2004).

18. Ibid.

A Successful Promotional Campaign: We Can't Keep Quiet About Our Electronic Resources

Sian Brannon

INTRODUCTION

The Denton Public Library is a growing system of three branches located approximately 35 minutes north of the Dallas/Fort Worth metroplex. The library shares the town of Denton with two state universities, as well as a growing number of senior retirement homes. There are about 106,000 people in our service area, and these residents are spread out over urban and rural communities. There is a need to supplement the print collection with electronic resources due to the growing computer savvy of everyone from schoolchildren to senior citizens.

The Denton Public Library's marketing campaign for electronic resources started by accident. While reviewing yearly statistics, I noticed an alarming trend in the decline of our patrons' use of electronic resources. The numbers were dropping steadily. Total views of full-text articles varied from over 13,000 to under 700 during one six-month period. For a small public library system, this is very noticeable and suspect.

After double-checking the statistics on the library's fifty databases, and looking at three or four years' worth of data, I saw the overall trend was that the numbers were heading down, slowly and surely. I knew to expect certain periods of low-usage. Summer months rarely yield high statistics for electronic resources; December is also traditionally low. The library's other statistics were great: circulation was high, door counts were up, and reference transactions were rising. The time had come to pay attention to our databases. The idea for the campaign was simple: "We Can't Keep Quiet About our Electronic Resources!" The library had been quiet for too long; it was time to make everyone aware of their existence.

Why hadn't the electronic resources been a focus before then? Public libraries pay thousands of dollars each year to provide these varied sources to their patrons, yet often they don't set aside money to promote them. We supposedly utilize the same collection development policies in evaluating, selecting, and retaining electronic resources as we do our print collections. In some libraries, electronic resources have virtually replaced print reference collections. For the Denton Public Library, there had been a period of approximately five years of expansion, remodeling,

37

and personnel realignment. After this settled down, the collections could become more of a focal point. First up: electronic resources.

MAKING SOME DECISIONS

I knew why I wanted to promote the databases–spending over $30,000 a year on a product is too much to be overlooked for so long. That part was simple. This fact alone made administration supportive of the campaign. Now what I had to decide was to whom and how should these electronic resources be marketed. To answer the first question, I queried library staff about their use of the databases in providing reference assistance to patrons. Not surprisingly, many reported that they were a "last resort" source. This was due to three things: a lack of knowledge regarding the contents of the electronic resources, a lack of knowledge of how to access what the resources offered, and a fear of teaching the public. These discoveries made answering the "who" questions simple. The library needed to focus on staff education first. You cannot promote a product you don't understand. Patrons will trust confident, knowledgeable staff more, and find more satisfaction in their use of the library with proper assistance.

Once the staff felt more comfortable with the electronic resources, which patrons would benefit most from knowing about them? Again, this seemed obvious–students. Being situated in a town with two universities and a growing number of high schools, it was natural to want to promote these resources to a group of people who would put them to high use. Who does that leave? I decided the last focus of our campaign would be to educate others in the community who weren't aware that databases could assist them with their everyday needs. It was time to move forward with the plan.

How would it happen? I thought I could undertake the education of staff with little assistance and low financial support, but I knew that some funding would be needed to help promote resources to the public. I also had to decide on a timeline, a method of advertising, and how to fit a marketing campaign in with all of the library's other ongoing programs. I had never done this before; exactly what was I going to do? I wasn't sure at the beginning, so I decided to work on as much staff education as I could while figuring out the rest of the steps.

SMART STAFF = SMART PATRONS

A good portion of our databases are provided through the TexShare Database Program of the Texas State Library and Archives Commission. The program's Web site, www.texshare.edu, provides many helpful tutorials and instructional materials on how to operate specific databases and information on how to conduct research in general. Beginning here, I compiled a Microsoft Word document with a brief description of each database we provided, its general purpose and contents, and any helpful search tips. This extensive document gave me a starting point for educating my co-workers–for free!

Each week I e-mailed a portion of my database document to staff. I included all staff, from clerks in Circulation to the director. Every person who came in contact with a library patron, or potential library patron, needed to have some knowledge of the services we provided. All I asked of staff each week was that they read the e-mail about one particular database (or small group of resources), go to the computer, and try a search or two. Now they had at least a brief glimpse of the contents and the interface of the database.

Granted, to send a summary of each individual database that we owned to staff weekly would have taken around a year. Not having that kind of time, I condensed some resources with similar interfaces (like EBSCO or Gale products) into one e-mail. I also skipped a few of the more specialized databases, such as those covering genealogy or auto repair, and instead included these in a list of topics that the databases covered. I planned to address them more specifically in face-to-face classes.

Luckily, my library has a computer lab that can be reserved for class training. Twenty staff members at a time can each sit at computers while watching a demonstration on a projector. Administration was happy to have free training provided for the staff and was supportive in allowing staff to take time to teach and attend these sessions. Usually taking less than one hour, I would introduce a group of databases based on the types of reference questions I had received that week. For example, one session might include an introduction to our auto-repair resource and Infotrac; the next session would focus solely on literature resources. Varying the subject matter and using specific examples of real-life reference questions allowed the staff to maintain interest and gave them incentive to practice on their own. If you do not have a lab environment for training, try using one computer and a smaller number of staff.

In addition to classes taught by library staff, we took advantage of free education provided by the Texas State Library. Occasionally there would be classes in the local area that staff were permitted to attend, covering the EBSCO interface, the TexShare databases in general, or finding government information. One of the local universities, which just happens to have a library science program, started an online training program covering various library science topics for a fee of less than $10 per class. I planned to make use of this "Library Education @ Your Desktop" program for more formal electronic-resource training for the staff.

There probably will always be some staff who just "don't get" electronic resources. They may be computer-illiterate, stuck in the old (print) ways of reference, or just dead-set against them. Try coaching these staff one-on-one, but remember that you can't help everyone. Try to at least make these staff aware that the resources exist, and show them how they function. You can't force them to use electronic resources in their reference transactions, but if a patron has a question about how to use one, at least they can assist.

By educating the staff first, we were able to place a little incentive into the campaign. Rewards were to be given monthly to the branch with the biggest increase in usage of electronic resources. These rewards ranged from pizza parties to having staff from other branches come to help shelve. At the end of the projected timeline of a year, overall winners could expect a special party, or perhaps a visit from Administration to do their shelving and public service deskwork.

SHOW ME THE MONEY

The next phase of our electronic resources awareness project was to promote the resources to our patrons. We realized we would need additional funds to implement this promotional campaign and began to search for external funding. We found that there are many places to find money for libraries. Sometimes it doesn't seem like it, but if one looks around long enough, it is generally possible to obtain funding. When developing a funding proposal, you must be able to explain specifically what it is for, and how the use of the money will benefit the library and its patrons. Prepare a budget of what you estimate materials will cost, or better yet, get quotes from specific companies. Clearly define each step of your implementation plans.

Start close to home when looking for funding for a campaign such as this. First, ask Administration if any money is budgeted for promotional materials and training. If there isn't, or if there isn't enough, try asking your Friends of the Library group for help. Perchance there are some local businesses that would be interested in partnering with you–try asking at the Chamber of Commerce in your area. Consult your state library association for possible grants and funding sources, including research assistance funding. If your state or geographic area is broken up into regional library systems, ask them as well.

We obtained a relatively small "awareness" grant from the North Texas Regional Library System that was designed to help libraries with promotions assistance. The grants are awarded regularly for demonstration of planning and indicators of positive outcomes for the community. The grant was originally intended to provide for the hiring of a consultant for marketing guidance, but was amended to include marketing projects that did not include outside consultation. Our project was selected in 2005 and we were awarded $2500 to fund our campaign. The application (Appendix A) was simple as far as grant applications go, but it is a good example of what to expect at a minimum. It includes the answers we gave in our application. A quick summary of the budget for the proposed marketing plan is in Appendix B.

To apply for the grant, I came up with a budget that included estimated costs for promotional materials I would purchase. One of the goals of the project was to insure that each student in the local middle and high schools became familiar with our catchphrase: "We Can't Keep Quiet About our Electronic Resources!" How could we do this and stay within budget?

PROMOTIONAL MATERIALS SEEM FUN . . .

Everyone has opinions–and most people like to share them. The easiest way to find out what type of promotional incentive a student in high school would use was to ask around. After querying the staff for their idea of the perfect giveaway, I asked almost every tween and teen that came into the library for a few days what type of item could they use, and what would they use often? I had some things in mind from looking through catalogs, but was surprised to find out that the "cool" items that I had selected, such as water bottles or rulers, were not as popular as I had hoped. The items most frequently mentioned were also the most basic–pens and pencils. Students ALWAYS need pens and pencils. Also, and this worked out in my favor, they are relatively inexpensive.

Fortunately, the North Texas Regional Library System offers more services than just awareness grants. They proffered my library the use of their magnet-making machine, and also designed a logo for the magnets. We were given supplies for 5000 magnets; the catch being that we had to assemble them ourselves. No problem! Librarians are notorious for scrounging around for free stuff, and this was no exception.

While coworkers dutifully assembled magnet after magnet, I inquired of several companies for quotes on pen and pencil printing. Note that in my budget, I asked for money for rulers and magnets. Rulers were relatively inexpensive, but as I said earlier, turned out not to be popular. I was permitted to spend the money on a substitute product, then incorporate the money designated for magnets into this as well. After choosing a vendor based on price, I submitted my orders. The vendor provided a time estimate for delivery, and worked with my municipality on setting up a purchase order.

Another budget item stated that we would spend 20% of the allocated funds on printed materials. We all know that patrons tend not to notice many of our signs, so I needed something that would stand out, attract attention, and offer the briefest hint of what electronic resources are all about. Another librarian and I decided to create a double-sided, 1/4 page "quick reference card" that would be economical, even when printed on cardstock. It included topics covered by our resources, and also showed who was paying for them. It contained a rough definition of databases in hopes of swaying some of the students and teachers who swear that they cannot use databases because they are not permitted to use Internet resources (see Figures 1-2).

We now had promotional materials with slogans, but what about real advertising? We had no real budget for advertising, so we needed to

FIGURE 1. Promotional Handout, page 1

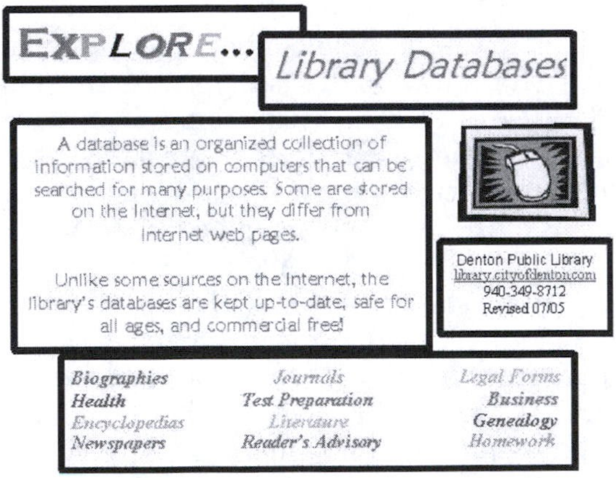

Used with permission.

FIGURE 2. Promotional Handout, page 2

Some databases are available
only inside the library:
　*Reference USA
　*Ancestry Plus
　*Law Check
　*Biography Reference Bank
　*Books in Print
Some databases are accessible over
the Internet from anywhere with a
library card!
　*NetLibrary
　*LearningExpressLibrary

Ask us how on your next visit!

TeXShare Databases
Business Source Premier
Regional Business News
Health & Wellness Center
Handbook of Texas
WorldCat
MedLine
Master File Premier
Heritage Quest Online
Texas Sanborn Maps
Student Resource Center
Academic Search Premier
Infotrac Custom Newspapers
Contemporary Authors
Contemporary Literary Criticism
Literature Resource Center

The TexShare databases are intended for use by customers
of the Denton Public Library. They are made possible
through the Texas State Library and Archives Commission
with the Telecommunications Infrastructure Fund Board.

think "home-grown." The first obvious choice was to include promotions of various resources in our regular monthly newspaper advertisement. Then we included these same promotions in e-mails to patrons that had volunteered their e-mail addresses to the library for regular updates of library happenings. Next, we added a line mentioning the electronic resources to our outgoing automated phone calls reminding people about holds that needed to be picked up or overdue materials. We added the same line as an introduction to our message for all incoming calls handled by the automated telephone system. To attract customers who normally relied on print resources, we established "Want to find more on (subject here)? Try the (electronic resources here)!" signs interspersed through the stacks. For example, next to our Chilton's repair manuals for cars, is a sign for the electronic version (see Figure 3).

ON TO THE PUBLIC

Staff were coming along on knowing about our electronic resources, and after being through a little training and a lot of exposure, felt more comfortable using them to answer reference questions. We had selected promotional products and printed informational handouts. It was time to move on to the education of the public.

FIGURE 3. Sample Advertisement

Auto Repair?

**If you can't find the
book you need, try
our Auto Repair
database. Ask how
at the reference desk.**

Since one of the main groups who could potentially increase our database usage was students, we started there. Staff made visits to high schools to deliver pens, pencils, cards, and to offer classes to students in the libraries or classrooms. When the opportunity was not available to instruct students directly at the schools, we made sure to have a one-on-one sit-down with the school's librarian, where we gave them a formal training session and implored for help in educating teachers regarding the difference between Internet resources and electronic resources. We also attempted to gain admission to teachers' in-service days to formally educate them as well, but were not successful in obtaining any meetings.

Another good idea, in retrospect, would have been to visit the junior high schools as well. Time did not permit us to visit everyone that we would have liked, but we covered as much ground as possible at the time. We would also have liked to invite teachers to bring their students to the library during school hours for tours and instruction. Training the students in our facilities, as well as introducing them to our print collections, would have been a great opportunity for them.

In-house, we held multiple classes for the public introducing specific databases. We encouraged all the librarians to hold their own classes, demonstrating the electronic resource they were most familiar with. They were required to target publicity to specific patrons and to get the word out themselves. It was easy to round up a few patrons for an introduction to some of our more interesting resources like e-books, test preparation, or genealogical databases, but we struggled trying to convey the importance of the periodicals resources, the Thomas Register, or the more complicated government databases.

Aside from teaching the general classes, a conscious decision needed to be made by staff to show off their newly-refreshed electronic resource skills in their reference transactions. Now that they were more aware of the contents and functionality of the resources, they should be using them in their day-to-day operations. Not only must they be attempting to answer reference questions with them, but they should also be trying to instruct the public as well. We were already doing this with our print resources, pointing out the indexes and indicating how to use the online catalog to locate items of interest, but it was difficult for some staff to transfer the idea of instruction to electronic resources. They didn't feel comfortable with their own skills, let alone confident in demonstrating search techniques to patrons. The inclusion of the aforementioned incentives did help this situation, but it was a difficult transition for some staff to make from using the traditional print materials to electronic resources.

The promotional materials, imprinted with our slogan "We Can't Keep Quiet About Our Electronic Resources!" did come in handy. We purchased them with the intention of giving them all away, so every time someone asked to borrow a pen or a pencil, we would say "You can have it! Ask if you'd like me to show you how to use the databases." Or, "Sure, it's yours to keep. We have new electronic resources available, if you'd like, I can show you the (___database.)" Any time we had a parent or child doing homework, we would give them an informational card and tell them that we had many more resources than we could fit into the building. We also informed people that they could access most of them from home. Given the opportunity, we showed people how to log-on from their personal computers.

STARTING OVER

Staff come and go. So do electronic resources. One exceedingly important concept of a campaign is to keep it going. New staff need to be indoctrinated to the importance of using and promoting electronic resources. Staff also need to be made aware of the acquisition and elimination of these resources. Costs change, vendors drop resources, and new products become available. These constant changes need to be addressed in the campaign. Although the program is started with a timeline in mind, and a general goal of promoting the resources, the promotion never ends.

At the beginning of the campaign, we had a set plan and budget. As it turns out, you cannot always stick to the proposed plan. We changed the promotional materials we intended to purchase; we found alternate sources for some products, and we changed methods of training. All of this affected the budget. Keeping your funding authority aware of these changes is the best practice.

We are almost out of promotional materials. Though there is no intention of purchasing more with library funds, there is always a chance that we can find more outside funding. Even if we do not, we still are able to make copies of our promotional cards with regular library supplies, and we can still educate the public and ourselves for free. The focus for the next year will be to contact the electronic resource vendors and see what materials they can provide. We will continue to visit local schools to talk with teachers and librarians.

WHAT WE ACCOMPLISHED

At first glance, it may seem difficult to include a marketing campaign, even as small as this particular one was, in with all of your library's other regular programming, instruction, and basic services. If I had considered that before starting on this campaign, I believe I would have had second thoughts. On the other hand, the aspects of this campaign are not that far removed from regular everyday library services. We highlight new print collections with displays–we highlight the electronic resources with promotional materials. We conduct outreach visits and perform storytimes; we also now provide outreach instruction sessions for these resources. Libraries use advertising to spread the word about new children's programming and upcoming new DVD releases. We can make use of these same media outlets to spread the word about electronic resources. We try to give our customers more resources than they think they might need while conducting reference transactions; the electronic resources are one more convenient method of answering reference questions. The extra commitment allows you to promote another wonderful, and very expensive, collection and to allow patrons to experience your library in new ways.

The campaign was not only successful in raising database usage statistics, but it was popular with staff and library users. It built teamwork and enthusiasm among the staff. It also helped to reaffirm the library's role as the center of lifelong learning in the community, and serves as a model for others to follow. Furthermore, the campaign aided the library in forming new, and strengthening existing, community partnerships. We maintained close contact with our Friends of the Library group, gave classes on business resources to the Chamber of Commerce, and certainly strengthened our bond with the local high schools. Overall, marketing our electronic resources showed us that we could maintain this type of activity in addition to providing regular library services, secure positive publicity within a small budget, and improve our reputation as a city asset offering a variety of resources.

APPENDIX A
Grant Application

1. Is this a continuation of last year's library awareness mini-grant project?

No.

2. Tell about your community. Where is it located? Is your community rural, suburban or urban?

The city of Denton is located approximately 35 miles north of Dallas and Fort Worth at the junction of Interstate Highways 35E and 35W. Denton is a diverse community with a current population of 90,200 that is projected to increase to 181,015 by 2025 (North Central Texas Council of Governments). According to the 2000 Census, Denton's fastest growing population is of Hispanic origin, represented by 16.4% of the population. In addition to the Hispanic community, the city's diverse population is reflected by the following percentages: 76% White, 9% Black, 3% Asian, 12% all other.

With a current population of 432,976 (2000 Census), Denton County is one of the fastest growing counties in the state. It is expected to increase its population by 127% by the year 2020. From 1990 to 1999, the population of the city of Denton grew by 13.6% while Denton County grew by 46.6% (North Texas Council of Governments). Because the Denton Public Library is open to all residents in the county, this significant increase in population will have a large impact on library collections and services.

The Denton Public Library has recently expanded to three locations in order to keep up with the growing demands. The Emily Fowler Central Library is in the downtown area in a historic building that is currently being renovated, and is due to reopen in June, 2005. The South Branch Library, opened in 1995, serves the south part of the city, while the recently opened North Branch Library serves the north side. Since many of the small Denton County communities do not have access to a public library, their citizens rely on Denton Public Library for services.

3. Project description: What is it you wish to market? To whom? Tell about your library's need to market to this group(s).

The funds requested in this proposal, $2,500.00, will allow the library to initiate a campaign to publicize the many electronic resources provided by the library and the Texas State Library. Currently the Denton Public Library records low usage statistics of these databases. A campaign involving pamphlets, media exposure, staff training, website reconstruction, and public classes would help turn those statistics around.

Not only will library staff profit from increased knowledge of electronic resources, many users in the community will benefit as well. Homeschooled children, students, teachers, genealogists, and business people are just a few examples of community members who stand to gain information and improve from learning about reliable non-Internet information.

By publicizing the existence, versatility, ease of access, and benefits of the library's electronic resources, the Denton Public Library hopes to change the perceptions of our users and turn them into electronic resources users and supporters.

The goals of this campaign are:

- Increase awareness of electronic resources to existing users who are unaware of all the library has to offer
- Increase awareness of electronic resources to the non-library user in the general public
- Develop and distribute to the public products which promote electronic resources [Examples: slogans, Public Service Announcements, press releases, and printed materials, training classes, websites]
- Partner with community educational institutions, such as the school district and Denton Homeschool Association, to discuss educational attributes of databases
- Collaborate with businesses and service groups in the community to promote library usage

4. List positive outcomes this project will have on your library.

The Denton Public Library predicts that the following outcomes will result from this campaign:

- Provide for an increased awareness of the library as a whole
- Take library services out into the community
- Connect the library through partnerships with other community organizations
- Allow the library to continue to meet expanding research needs under budget constraints
- Furnish staff with exposure to a variety of resources, thus making for a more educated workforce

5. List positive outcomes this project will have on your community.

The Denton Public Library predicts that this campaign will benefit our community through the following outcomes:

- Provide information services for the community's personal decisions
- Give the community access to high-quality information resources
- Help establish the library as a center of lifelong learning within the community
- Promote library awareness, thus making it attractive not only to current residents, but also to prospective residents and businesses

6. How can the library awareness consultant help you? Describe the role of the library awareness consultant. (If you are not using a consultant, you may omit this requirement.)

N/A.

7. If you are doing your project in-house without the services of an outside consultant, you must submit a detailed budget. How much will you spend on books? On copy paper? On postage? If you are producing a library awareness videotape, what costs will be involved?

APPENDIX B
Grant Application Summary Budget

Category	Item	Price
Printing	Pamphlets/Flyers/Quick Reference Cards	$500.00
Promotional Materials & Advertising	Rulers for middle & high school students (8000 @ $.15)	$1200.00
	Magnets (5000 @ $.12)	$600.00
	Website promotions	FREE
	Emails to patrons and community members	FREE
	Presentations to public	FREE
Training	Online staff training workshops in databases provided by the University of North Texas Library Education @ Desktop program	$200.00
Total		$2500.00

Marketing to Community College Users

Mark S. Thompson
Lynn Schott

INTRODUCTION

Marketing electronic resources (e-resources) to the users of community college libraries is a challenge because of their student populations. Given the emphasis on open enrollment and low tuition, community colleges serve a student body with a very diverse range of educational and cultural backgrounds, including those without adequate formal education. This diversity means that the tasks of creating awareness of e-resources and increasing their usage are not straightforward efforts. Some of the students may be unfamiliar with library databases or may not appreciate their value as research tools. Given these factors, a key management question exists: "We are spending a lot of time and money on electronic resources, but are the students taking full advantage of them?" Often the answer to this question at community colleges is no.

This situation demands assessment, creative action, and on-going marketing efforts. Given heavy demand at service desks and a busy library instruction schedule, the need for more formal efforts at marketing and assessment for e-resources may go unaddressed. This chapter presents some practical solutions to this challenge that were undertaken at two large community colleges in New Jersey. After careful consideration, both colleges conducted formal assessment efforts. The findings led to new insights and to changes to the marketing of e-resources. These changes ultimately proved successful in improving awareness and increasing usage of library e-resources. The two community colleges are the Union County College (UCC), which is located on four campuses, and serves a largely urban, lower middle class population in central New Jersey; and Bergen Community College (BCC), which is located on one campus and serves a largely suburban, higher-income county in northern New Jersey. UCC has about 12,000 and BCC about 15,000 full- and part-time students.

To start with, both college libraries had concluded that their student populations were not taking full advantage of e-resources. This was based on perspectives gathered from reference questions, at library instruction sessions, and in discussions with teaching faculty. However, a concerted effort to assess awareness or usage had not been undertaken before, so research was done to quantify awareness and the need for eresources. For the first time, usage statistics were collected to assess demand.

As a result of the assessments, the libraries identified under-utilized e-resources and took new approaches to marketing them. Both college libraries also developed a process to track database usage statistics, so the impact of any marketing efforts could be measured over time. Analysis of the statistics showed that increased usage was observed as a result of several initiatives undertaken by the colleges, including using database pathfinders, revamping the library Web site, changing which databases were covered in library instruction sessions, and conducting workshops aimed at faculty.

CASE STUDY #1:
BERGEN COMMUNITY COLLEGE (BCC)

At Bergen Community College, e-resources and the library instruction program had expanded along with a growing student population. No formal marketing plan was in effect, but library assessment became an important issue as an outgrowth of its Middle States Commission on Higher Education accreditation review. An assessment plan was developed by the library and a full-scale customer satisfaction survey (LibQUAL)[1] was conducted to identify areas of need. After analyzing the data, marketing e-resources emerged as one of the needs. In addition, new financial pressures emerged as the cost of e-resources increased and the funding sources became threatened. The reference staff needed to make decisions about cancelling, renewing or buying new databases. Therefore, it became imperative to know which databases were used and how much they were used.

Identifying Usage Patterns at BCC: Background

The core of assessing the success of marketing e-resources is the usage statistics of those resources. Without a full-time electronic services librarian or any formal marketing plan, no complete baseline of usage for all the e-resources had been captured at BCC. Once BCC did attempt to capture the complete picture of usage, however, they found it was not a straightforward process. First, not all e-resource vendors provided usage statistics. Second, many of the vendors required an administrator to log into a remote service to download the statistical information, which was a time-consuming task. Thirdly, most admin sites post data monthly, often on a delayed schedule, so that twelve months of current data were difficult to collect.

Fortunately, many vendors have recently begun to offer the means to have reports delivered via e-mail as text, .HTML, or .CSV (comma-de-limited) files suitable for importing into Microsoft Excel, or a similar spreadsheet. Although the files are delivered automatically, compiling the data remains a labor-intensive process. This process is also prone to error, since many vendors do not record their statistics in a uniform manner. Some have adopted the Project Counter standard reports,[2] but many vendors continue to use their own vocabulary and accounting methods. Usage reports list terms such as: "visits," "activities," "views," "retrievals," and "requests."

In Figure 1, you see a sample summary table pulled from the administrative module for one of the e-resource vendor sites. Note the use of the terms "estimated hits" (results list) and "content views" (full-text), along with the more universal terms "searches" and "sessions." The table shows results from tabulations done in the administrative module of World Book Online, listing total BCC usage for a one-year period from both on-campus and remote access usage. Note the large variation by month reflecting the cycle of courses, assignments and papers during the academic year.

FIGURE 1. Sample Vendor Statistics Output

Main Account View–BERGEN COMMUNITY COLLEGE				
Month*	Estimated Hits	Product Sessions	Content Views	Searches
Jul 2005	2,140	16	43	48
Aug 2005	1,140	7	31	19
Sep 2005	2,700	37	70	28
Oct 2005	29,960	139	915	444
Nov 2005	22,100	107	636	362
Dec 2005	9,780	82	215	192
Jan 2006	900	18	12	15
Feb 2006	33,840	197	846	649
Mar 2006	39,120	230	955	771
Apr 2006	37,460	224	865	784
May 2006	8,240	73	131	208
Jun 2006	10,320	49	281	186
12 Months Total	197,700	1,179	5,000	3,706
* Sorted Column.				

Source: World Book Online admin site. Used with permission.

Identifying Usage Patterns at BCC: Data Compilation and Analysis

Finally, after much work, BCC was able to compile a summary of usage from most of its databases over a period of one academic year (July through June). The sample below in Figure 2 shows an extract of the table that ranks databases by total number of searches conducted during July 2004-June 2005. Similar data was collected for the total sessions and the total full-text requests. The table shows 11 of the most-used and 7 of the lesser-used databases. Note the large differences by database title. Total usage by title ranges from a low of only 130 per year up to 79,724 per year. In reviewing its baseline of database usage statistics, BCC came to several basic conclusions:

FIGURE 2. Total Number of Searches by Database (July 2004-June 2005)

Database	Total
Expanded Academic ASAP Plus	79,724
Academic Search Premier	35,787
Literature Resource Center	32,519
CJPI	28,622
Lexis-Nexis	27,867
17ABI/Hoover's/WSJ through ProQ	25,413
PA Research II	23,974
Ethnic NewsWatch	23,817
PsycArticles (EBSCO)	8,167
Science Direct	7,110
CINAHL	4,730
.	
.	
.	
Philosopher's Index	531
Grove Music Online	502
Gale Virtual Reference Libr.	501
Communication & Mass Media (CMMC)	479
Grove Art Online	478
American Humanities Index	417
Mergent Online	130
Total	327,826

Source: Bergen Community College, internal. Used with permission.

1. The multi-disciplinary databases, like Academic Search Premier, were used heavily, but the specialized databases, such as Grove Art Online and Mergent Online, were rarely used.
2. To adequately understand usage of specific database titles, multi-year statistics were needed to determine trends.
3. To understand low usage, one must review all possible underlying causes and focus on the key issues effecting usage levels.

Assessing Awareness at BCC: Overall

Armed with database statistics, BCC now wanted to see if demand was low in some areas because of lack of awareness. With a community college audience, it is best not to assume that students are aware of the library subscription databases. Fortunately, at Bergen Community College, a formal, quantitative survey, LibQUAL, was conducted among its users which included questions on e-resources and marketing issues.

When the results came back, the assumptions proved true–students were poorly informed about available e-resources and had difficulty accessing them. Three key issues on the survey that related to finding and learning about e-resources received low ratings on the expected and/or perceived levels of service:

- "Making me aware of library resources and services."
  - 30% of students ranked it below their minimum expected level of service.
- "A library Web site enabling me to locate information on my own."
  - The perceived level of service for this issue was rated the lowest among 28 core issues on the survey.
- "Easy-to-use access tools that allow me to find things on my own."
  - Rated barely above the minimum expected level of service by students.

These ratings pointed to the need for improvements in the library Web site and in marketing efforts for e-resources. These issues were further clarified in follow-up interviews and discussions. This work revealed that students clearly knew they needed articles to complete their research assignments; how to find them was a mystery. Library instruction sessions were adequately training students on specific databases to complete their assignments. Apparently the problem was more basic–students walking into the library often had trouble finding the right resources via the library

Web site. From the library homepage, students were confused about where to find articles and how to select databases by title or subject.

Assessing Awareness at BCC: Library Web site

A project to assess and overhaul the library Web site was undertaken, including usability research on the current, and then on the re-designed, Web pages. Almost immediately, the assessment effort provided surprising insights. Usability research was conducted in three phases (initial audit, detailed review of old pages, and testing of new pages) involving students, faculty and staff. The usability testing was conducted informally, on an ad hoc basis. A test server was used to host draft versions of the new pages.

Benchmarking of other library Web sites was done to find how other libraries handled portrayal of e-resources on their Web sites. Articles were found that named specific sites as good examples of easy-to-use library Web sites. Books on Web usability guidelines were reviewed (see Bibliography) and proved to be valuable, especially *Don't Make Me Think* by Steve Krug. The Krug book became the key guide for how to conduct testing and it was used as the basis for usability guidelines. The most useful usability testing came from the one-on-one sessions with students, either as they approached a library workstation or as they were leaving a computer. The focus of the sessions varied from navigation, testing the ability to complete tasks, or trialing specific page functions. The sessions were kept short–a total of only five to ten minutes each. Many students declined to participate, as they were too busy to help, but many did agree. Longer sessions were conducted among small groups of students assembled from among library student aides, Student Technology Consultants (student computer lab workers), and Student Ambassadors (peer assistance aides).

The working hypothesis proved correct: many users found the old library Web pages somewhat cumbersome to use for locating e-resources. The depictions of databases were poor, so the extent of the e-resources content or how to distinguish among them was not clear. In the old site, it took at least four clicks to get into an actual database. Even students or faculty who had previously used a database were sometimes unable to find it again. Changes in the Web site design were clearly needed.

Changing the Marketing Approach at BCC: Web site

Once again BCC was fortunate, since college administration had already decided to migrate all college Web sites to a new Web software platform. The library took this opportunity to change not only its e-resources pages, but the flow and content of the entire library Web site. During the re-design process, librarians worked with students, internal staff and faculty to shape a site that delivered clearly understood, easily accessible content. It became clear that the library homepage was an important marketing tool that guided users to resources in the library. Early discussions with users and reviews of other library sites suggested that a "one-stop shopping" approach might better serve users. This led to the complete revamp of the library homepage. Three "jumping-off points" were created directly on the homepage that let students perform their three most performed tasks: searching the online catalog, searching for articles, and searching the Internet. In fact, each of these areas was renamed with student-focused language: Find Books, Find Articles, and Find on the Web (see www.bergen.edu/library).

In assessing the old e-resource pages, the team realized that the Web site design forced students to make step-by-step decisions about what information they wanted. This allowed for a "clean" page with minimal links, but added a level of aggravation to returning users who wanted to reduce their number of mouse clicks. Figure 3 illustrates the navigation flow in the old Web site. Users needed to open the library homepage, find and click on the Electronic Resources link on the homepage, then select the list they wanted, and then click the link for the database title in order to see a search box.

Another central issue that came to light was the sheer number of online databases, which had grown to over eighty. It was no longer helpful to simply provide a long alphabetical list of titles with groupings under various categories. As illustrated in Figure 4, the selection tool was confusing for users and necessitated multiple clicks. Also, it was clear that listing databases on static pages (as had been done) was not efficient. The old design listed many of the databases on multiple pages, and any change to a URL or description had to be altered on a number of individual pages (by subject, by title, etc.).

With the help of the college Web Development Team, a new e-resources table was constructed with a dynamic interface to a set of e-resources. The new page allowed users to sort databases by title or subject area. The table was created "on-the-fly"–in other words, the user could click a sort button and have the table re-sorted by subject or title. A simple alphabet listing allowed users to jump ahead in the list to titles in that letter. Each database title had its own brief description, rather than having simple lists on one page and descriptions on separate subpages. See

FIGURE 3. Sample Navigational Flow for E-Resources Pages on BCC Web Site

Home Page Links (pre-2005)

- Library Catalog
- Electronic Resources ➜
- General Library Information
- Services for Students, Faculty & Staff

Electronic Resources Page Links

- Frequently Used Resources ➜
- Resources by Title
- Resources by Subject
- Internet Sites by Subject
- Librarians' Handouts
- Reference Works Online

Frequently Used Resources Page Links

- Academic Index ➜ Starts Selected Database
- Academic Search Premier
- Lexis-Nexis Academic
- MasterFILE Premier
- ProQuest Research Library

Source: Bergen Community College, internal. Used with permission.

FIGURE 4. View of the BCC Database List, Before the Redesign

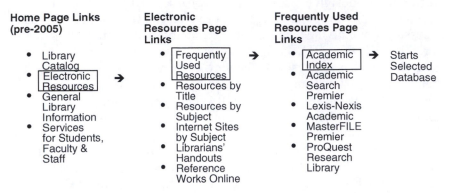

Source: Bergen Community College Web Pages, 2004. Used with permission.

the screen shot in Figure 5 with the new format to access e-resources or try it for yourself (www.bergen.edu/library/findarticles).

Also, with the dynamic table, changes to a specific database title could now be done from one table in an administrative mode, rather than the cumbersome process of editing page after page of information.

The sample page in Figure 5 shows the beginning of the alphabetical listing of databases. Note the ability to support a description along with name and subject for each database entered in the table.

All of this development was completed by the end of summer 2005 and then launched for the start of the fall 2005 semester. These changes were announced in a "welcome back" letter distributed to library patrons upon their arrival. It was also advertised to faculty using an e-mail newsletter called *Library Alert*. Flyers showing features of the new library Web site were distributed in the library.

FIGURE 5. View of the BCC Database List, After the Redesign

Find Articles/Electronic Resources

START with a Frequently Used Database:

Academic Search Premier | Expanded Academic ASAP Plus
Lexis-Nexis Academic | ProQuest Research Library

OR sort by: TITLE | SUBJECT

Off-Campus access to databases licensed by the Sidney Silverman Library is restricted to BCC faculty and staff and to students currently enrolled in courses which bear institutional and/or degree credits. For more information see: Remote Access/Restrictions

A | B | C | D | E | F | G | H | I | J | K | L | M | N | O | P | Q | R | S | T | U | V | W | X | Y | Z

A

Name	Description	Subject
ABI/Inform Complete	Index and full text database. Business, management, and industry publications. **	Business
ABYZ News Links	Links to news and broadcast stations around the world. Find news links by continent, region, country. Codes indicate the language of the linked site.	Newspapers
Academic Search Premier	Multi-disciplinary full text database. This scholarly collection offers information in: computer sciences, engineering, physics, chemistry, language and linguistics, arts & literature, medical sciences, ethnic studies, and many more. The majority of full text titles are available in PDF or scanned-in-color. * **	General

Source: Bergen Community College Web Pages, Sept. 2005. Used with permission.

Toward the end of the fall 2005 term, feedback forms were developed and distributed to users in order to capture input on the changes. Usability discussions continued through the beginning of the next term. Some small changes were made as a result of this feedback.

Results and Impact at BCC

At BCC, the revamp of the Web site to increase clarity and ease of use was successful. The evidence came from reference desk interactions and a feedback form. The feedback form questions were simply structured as:

About our upgraded Library Web site and online catalog:
   Was your use of the online catalog successful today?
   Was your use of the Library Web site successful today?

Both of these questions netted results of nearly 75 percent as YES votes. The comments received back included many that confirmed the re-design efforts were successful, including:

- *"It was easy to use."*
- *"You're doing a wonderful job."*
- *"I really like the look of it."*

Follow-up one-on-one interviews and other usability testing also netted positive feedback. Faculty, staff and students all liked the new pages. As for the e-resources pages, they now found databases more easily and using the new table made them more aware of what e-resources were available. Two further improvements were made to the layout of the e-resource pages after launch. During the semester, faculty asked for direct links from the homepage to the online newspaper collections and to online encyclopedias. Also, library instruction had been changed to focus on the newly renamed e-resource homepage ("Find Articles") and its table. Feedback from the librarians was positive.

The next step was to assess the success of using the Web site as the key marketing tool for e-resources. Had the new Web site impacted usage? Since BCC had a baseline for usage prior to the changes, the library could now measure post-implementation usage via the new web pages. BCC compiled these database statistics and compared the same period of time for the 2004 and 2005 academic years (pre- and post-Web changes).

Analysis of the numbers showed that there was a large increase in the Frequently Used Databases listed on the homepage. As seen in Figure 6, the greatest increase in use was for ProQuest Research Library (74.9%

increase in searches), followed by Academic Search Premier (65.6% increase in searches). Some of the specialized subject databases, which had been little used, showed large increases in use as well. Comparing 2004-2005 (July-June) with 2005-2006 (July-May), a sampling of the specialized databases showed increases in the total number of searches (51.75%), sessions (26.74%), and full-text retrievals (32.41%). There were individual drops in usage for some of these databases, but the overall volume was up.

What could explain these large increases? After discussion, the librarians eliminated enrollment as a cause, since it only increased 3 percent. Library instruction would not have driven demand, since total sessions were flat year to year. Since the new Web site had been widely marketed and used, it most likely accounted for the bulk of the increases. Special anomalies in the data were addressed. The most important of which was for the database, ARTstor, which increased by over 300 percent. This database benefited from both the Web change and a strong marketing effort by the library liaison. This librarian promoted and demonstrated ARTstor during library instruction classes and at a faculty conference workshop that fall. In addition, vendor demonstrations were arranged for interested faculty during the fall semester.

BCC concluded that the change in the Web site was successful in driving up usage, especially when used in conjunction with more traditional exposure during library instruction classes and through demonstrations to the faculty.

CASE STUDY #2:
UNION COUNTY COLLEGE (UCC)

Assessing Awareness at UCC

At UCC, the library went through a similar self examination as that of BCC. A review of questions at the Reference Desk revealed a low level of awareness of databases. The assistant director took on the task of analyzing database usage statistics, since none had previously been collected. Reviewing the set of database titles showed that usage was less than might be expected among several titles, including most of the specialized resources.

A review of methods utilized to inform students of e-resource was conducted. UCC had done some marketing of e-resources via a database handout that included descriptions and coverage. Since the total number of databases was small (only 39 separate titles), the Web site was straightforward in how it displayed the titles. The librarians real-

FIGURE 6. Comparison Data for (July-June) at Bergen Community College

Database		2004-2005	2005-2006*	% Change
Frequently Used Databases				
Academic Search Premier	Sessions	13,430	17,097	27.30
	Searches	35,787	59,268	65.61
Expanded Academic ASAP Plus	Sessions	28,884	14,172	−50.93
	Searches	79,724	34,787	−56.37
Lexis-Nexis	Sessions	N/A	N/A	N/A
	Searches	27,867	34,973	25.50
ProQuest Research Library	Sessions	13,841	18,558	34.08
	Searches	23,974	41,931	74.90
Total Sessions for Freq. Used		56,155	49,827	−11.27
Total Searches for Freq. Used		167,352	170,959	2.16
Selected Specialized Databases				
ARTstor	Sessions	329	872	165.05
	Searches	836	3,534	322.73
Biography Reference Bank	Sessions	507	571	12.62
	Searches	1,538	1,730	12.48
CINAHL	Sessions	1,759	1,838	4.49
	Searches	28,622	46,516	71.80
Criminal Justice Periodical Index	Sessions	13,841	18,558	34.08
	Searches	28,622	46,516	62.52
Grove Music Online	Sessions	298	146	−51.01
	Searches	502	249	−50.40
Magill On Literature	Sessions	656	1,134	72.87
	Searches	1,711	3,143	83.69
PsycArticles	Sessions	2,581	1,742	−32.51
	Searches	8,167	5,804	−28.93
World Book Online	Sessions	615	1,129	83.58
	Searches	2,484	3,513	41.43
Total Sessions for Selected Dbs.		20,995	26,609	26.74
Total Searches for Selected Dbs.		49,531	75,164	51.75

*BCC 2005-2006 (July-May). Used with permission.

ized that they primarily relied on library instruction sessions as a way to inform students about e-resources. For those students who did not attend a library instruction session, however, the library had to rely solely on teaching faculty to convey information about what library resources should be used by students to complete assignments.

Relying on library instruction as the primary marketing tool to reach faculty and students was a concern, since faculty requests for library instruction had been slow. The concern was echoed by the office of the Academic Vice President. He had recently launched a new initiative on library instruction as an outgrowth of concerns about the new standards issued by the Association of College and Research Libraries (ACRL) and the Middle States Commission on Higher Education regarding information literacy.

To understand the situation, a complete assessment of the UCC library instruction program was done to determine which departments and faculty members used library instruction. The Head of Instruction gathered the library class tallies from previous years and analyzed the patterns. The assessment results were alarming. Of most concern was the extent to which some academic areas were receiving no instruction. The English faculty dominated the users of library instruction–about 75 percent of all library instruction sessions conducted were for either credit English, developmental English or ESL (English as a Second Language). An additional concern surfaced. Since English library instruction classes were short and only the literature databases were discussed, students had little exposure to the other e-resources in the library. Literature databases represented only four of 39 databases that students would need during their college career.

With help from the institutional research office, an analysis of the curriculum at UCC was done to determine the number of students and staff in each of the program areas. This was mapped to what library instruction sessions were given. The results were clear. A high percentage of English classes were being reached. But besides English, only the psychology department was taking advantage of library instruction; and there, only adjuncts were bringing their classes in, not the long-time, tenured professors. Neglected almost completely were history, sociology, business, science, and allied health–all important programs at UCC, each enrolling hundreds of students.

UCC librarians reviewed other curricular areas where the faculty might make library skills a priority for their classes. The only other place was in UCC 101, the first-year college experience class. The first-year experience course was assessed and it was found that the majority of faculty teaching this one-credit class did not bring their classes to the library. This occurred despite the fact that the faculty-approved course outline required at least one visit to the library. Clearly, changes needed to be made.

Changing the Marketing Approach at UCC

After reviewing its analysis of the library instruction program, UCC devised a new approach toward marketing the classes and the e-resources that were demonstrated during the sessions. First, everyone at the Reference Desk was directed to distribute and have faculty complete library instruction request forms. These forms were, in themselves, marketing tools since they clearly stated the purpose of the library instruction and asked faculty to describe their assignment and the databases needed. This would help stimulate further discussions about the databases needed for the course.

Second, new ways of enlisting faculty to sign up for classes were devised. An online form was created and posted to the library Web site. This led to a more thorough review of the library instruction pages on the site. A number of changes were implemented to make library instruction resources more prominent (see www.ucc.edu/library).

Third, the library liaisons reviewed the database list and selected key databases to promote in their curriculum areas. They created short how-to guides which were then made into printed handouts and short online tutorials. The liaisons scheduled time at academic department meetings to present these databases. They mentioned the features or demonstrated databases to the faculty. This new outreach effort by library liaisons was well received by department chairs and by faculty.

In the library, a more concerted effort was also made to study which databases were discussed and how e-resources were being taught in each class. All librarians who taught library instruction met with the Head of Instruction to review objectives for library instruction sessions. Since class time allowed for demonstration of only two databases, the librarians devised ways to mention other databases. One of these ways was through new pathfinders which profiled e-resources on specific topics. In addition, all library instruction materials were placed on a new instruction page on the library Web site (see www.ucc.edu/library/InstructionandResearchGuides).

Fourth, some of the liaisons joined the college-wide Information Literacy Team, which consisted of administration and teaching faculty from a number of disciplines. The team's purpose was to investigate ways to integrate information literacy into the curriculum. A sub-team was formed to work on new ways to infuse library instruction into the core education curriculum and the honors program, both of which were being revised.

Fifth, a new marketing avenue was created in faculty workshops. New workshops were designed to offer faculty, both full- and part-time, the chance to see a demonstration and have hands-on practice with the databases. The assistant director created a new course on "Designing a Better Research Assignment" that proved popular on faculty development days. Course specific e-resources were introduced during this class.

And finally, further efforts were made to improve UCC 101, the freshman experience class. The syllabus was revised to further clarify the elements of library instruction that should be covered. Everyone agreed to focus on a careers assignment that would be used to develop all types of college skills from scheduling, to outlining, to conducting library research. A careers pathfinder was developed for this class and posted to the Web. This, along with online catalog and database skill exercises, were all placed on the UCC 101 section of the library instruction page on the library Web. And the most important step of all was made when UCC 101 was voted in by the faculty as a mandatory class. Now, all new incoming UCC students would be given library instruction, including exposure to the breadth of e-resources available.

Results and Impact at UCC

The changes made in the library instruction program at UCC netted some important results. A positive trend was captured in the fact that the diversity of classes exposed to library instruction increased after the marketing measures were introduced as described above. The work of the liaisons and the information literacy committee had been a valuable influence on others. In the 2004 school year, the number of classes requested in addition to the English department included:

- 21 psychology classes,
- 31 freshman experience classes and
- 10 paralegal classes.

Analysis also revealed that the total number of library instruction sessions increased by 12 percent over the previous year. During the 2004 school year, a total of 348 instructional sessions were given on three of the four UCC campuses. However, there was still a sizeable gap in some departments between the number of course sections and library instruction sessions. This was true for: history (1 session), business (3 sessions), and allied health (4 sessions). Despite the large presence of these disciplines on campus, awareness-building has not yet resulted in a large increase in instructional sessions requested in these areas.

As a side affect of the awareness-building of e-resources, the total number of reference questions also increased. Many of these reference interactions were follow-ups to the increased number of library instruction sessions. The total number of reference questions increased from 7,257 in 2000-2001 to 10,840 in 2003-2004–nearly a 50 percent increase!

An analysis of database usage statistics documented the impacts on usage. For the key databases, large increases were measured between 2003 and 2004:

- The number of searches on Gale databases increased more than 75 percent and the number of articles retrieved jumped 87 percent:
  - Literature Resource Center: 49,536 searches
  - Discovering Collection: 13,432 searches
  - Health and Wellness Resource Center: 11,770 searches
- On ProQuest databases, usage increased more than 300 percent
- On EBSCO databases, usage increased more than 100 percent

LESSONS LEARNED:
COLLECTING USAGE STATISTICS

Collecting usage statistics from library databases is a task in flux. Comparisons to academic norms or even past statistics can be difficult. If academic libraries were able to clearly translate their vendor usage statistics into more useful categories such as searches, sessions, and full-text requests, then useful comparisons could be drawn. These reporting categories are used by ACRL and LRC (Library Research Center) on the Academic Library Trends & Statistics Survey.[3] In reviewing the summary data, the two community colleges in this report were able to compare certain benchmarks to other community colleges, through the data reported by ACRL from the survey.

In addition to the data collected by ACRL, the UCC and BCC teams ran some alternative calculations to look for patterns in usage. The most interesting calculations are for searches, sessions and full-text requests per student per year. This data might be compared to the number of courses and assignments a student might have during a typical semester. Further work is needed to determine the potential value of these measurements.

As a start, Figure 7 shows a table that UCC created for the 2003-2004 school fiscal year. An enrollment of 11,058 students translates to 18.1 searches per student per year. Total searches were nearly 200,000, which is double the ACRL average for community colleges. Figure 8 shows a three-year comparison that BCC created. Although enrollments increased only 2.4 percent and 3.1 percent over the three-year period, total sessions and searches almost doubled. One should note that BCC rates above average for searches per login, but falls below the average for retrievals per login compared to other 2-year colleges.

In studying its database statistics for marketing clues, BCC gained some important marketing insights:

- At one time, the library featured a "Database of the Month" on its home page. When combined with baseline usage statistics, this might be an effective tool for measuring demand. Unfortunately, this practice was only implemented for a few months and no statistics were kept.
- The library has a "frequently used databases" list on its e-resource Web page with links to four of the most-used, multi-disciplinary databases. The library lists these e-resources in alphabetical order, which analysis shows clearly effects the level of usage. When Academic Index was renamed Expanded Academic ASAP Plus, it moved down in the list to the second position which resulted in changed usage. In 2004-2005, Academic Index had about 80,000 searches and Academic Search Premier 36,000 searches (see Figure 6). In 2005-2006, the renamed Expanded Academic ASAP Plus (in the second position) had 35,000 searches and Academic Search Premier (in the first position) climbed to 60,000 searches, reversing the previous year's search counts.
- Ethnic NewsWatch was identified as one of the top ten databases in usage, given the statistics on searches and sessions delivered by the vendor (ProQuest). The high level of use, though, did not make sense from the librarians' viewpoint at the reference desk or in the classroom. After investigating the data more thoroughly, BCC discovered that ProQuest counts broad searches as searches in the overall product (Research Library) and each of its separate databases, which in effect highly inflated Ethnic NewsWatch usage statistics.

CONCLUSIONS AND NEXT STEPS

As was stated in our premise, marketing e-resources to community colleges is not easy. However, with a concerted effort to assess, plan and market e-resources, significant change can be realized. The assessment efforts at BCC pointed to the need for easier-to-use Web pages and simplified access to the databases. A major re-design of the Web site was completed during the summer of 2005, which resulted in higher usage and greater satisfaction with using database resources by the end of the fall 2005 term.

FIGURE 7. UCC Database Usage Statistics (2003-2004 Fiscal Year)

2003-2004 fiscal year	UCC	ACRL Norm
Total database titles	39	204
Total student enrollment	11,058	6,219
Total sessions*	NA	43,271
Total searches	199,842	96,246
Total F/T retrievals	335,662	180,188
Searches per student per year	18.1	15.48
F/T retrievals per student per year	30.4	28.97

*Total number of sessions could not be compiled.
Source: ACRL, *2004 Academic Library Trends & Statistics for Carnegie Classification: Associate's Colleges*, p. 58, p. 69.

FIGURE 8. Bergen Community College Usage Statistics Summary (July-June)

	2003-2004	ACRL 2003-2004 Norm(a)	2004-2005	2005-2006
Total Student Enrollment	13,991	6,219	14,325	14,762
Total Sessions	90,959(b)	43,271	130,880	150,411
Total Searches	227,975	96,246	327,826	404,159
Total Full-Text Retrievals	144,615(c)	180,188	176,700	209,231
Sessions per Student	6.5	6.96	9.14	10.19
Searches per Student	16.29	15.48	22.88	27.38
Full-Text Retrievals per Student	10.34	28.97	12.34	14.17
Searches per login	2.51	2.2	2.5	2.69
Retrievals per login	1.59	4.2	1.35	1.39
Total Number of Databases (reporting statistics)	27	204	35	39

Source: Bergen Community College, internal.   Notes: a–2003-2004 fiscal; b–not all vendors report; c–missing data for 2003.
Source: ACRL, *2004 Academic Library Trends & Statistics for Carnegie Classification: Associate's Colleges*, p. 58, p.69.

Next, BCC wants to continue usability testing of its Web site and analyzing of database usage statistics. Furthermore, the library instruction program will be assessed, as UCC had done, to map sessions to academic departments and review which databases are demonstrated and mapped to curriculum areas.

The assessment efforts at UCC resulted in a clearer understanding of library instruction usage by academic departments. After launching several new initiatives (including faculty development workshops, Web site forms, and information literacy initiatives) requests for library instruction sessions increased dramatically and participation was more widely distributed among the academic departments. As a byproduct of these efforts, both reference questions and database usage increased. Next, UCC wants to update its Web site and increase the number of workshops offered to faculty.

NOTES

1. LibQUAL is a suite of survey tools offered through Texas A&M University and the Association of Research Libraries' Statistics and Measurements Program (see www.libqual.org).
2. Project Counter is a non-profit organization with a mission to unify methods of reporting e-resource usage statistics. Their Web site is www.projectcounter.org.
3. ACRL/ALA has published its 2004 Library Trends & Statistics Data (*Academic Library Trends & Statistics*. Chicago: Association of College and Research Libraries, 2005). Or go to the Web site: http://acrl.telusys.net/trendstat/2004/.

BIBLIOGRAPHY

Augustine, Susan and Courtney Greene. 2002. Discovering How Students Search a Library Website: A Usability Case Study. *College & Research Libraries.* 63 (4): 354-365.
Bucknall, Tim. 2005. Getting More from Your Electronic Collection Through Studies of User Behavior. *Against the Grain.* 17 (5): 1-20.
Cohen, Laura B. and Julie M. Still. 1999. A Comparison of Research University and Two-year College Library Websites: Content, Functionality, and Form. *College & Research Libraries.* 60 (3): 275-289.
Franklin, Brinley. 2005. Managing the Electronic Collection With Cost Per Use Data. *IFLA Journal.* 31 (3): 241-248.
Krug, Steve. 2000. *Don't Make Me Think: A Common Sense Approach to Web Usability.* Berkeley, CA: New Riders.
Nielsen, Jakob and Marie Tahir. 2002. *Homepage Usability: 50 Websites Deconstructed. 2002.* Berkeley, CA: New Riders.
Petrick, Joseph. 2002. Electronic Resources and Acquisitions Budgets: SUNY Statistics, 1994-2000. *Collection Building.* 21 (3): 123-133.
Schufreider, Bob. Value of Usage Statistics to Library Decision Making. 2006. In *Electronic Resources & Libraries Conference* 2006 (Georgia Institute of Technology). (see http://smartech.gatech.edu/handle/1853/10062).
Shorten, Jay. 2004. What Do Community College Libraries Do With Electronic Resources? *Community & Junior College Libraries.* 12 (2): 45-69.

Marketing Electronic Resources to Distance Students: A Multipronged Approach

Julia Leong

When students are surveyed regarding their expectations and satisfaction with library services, it is common to receive suggestions for services or guides the library might offer. In many cases these suggested services already exist. This has been shown to be true in surveys of distance students at the University of New England, Armidale, New South Wales, Australia (UNE). Distance students' varying, and often limited, knowledge of what their home institution offers, coupled with low expectations[1] and remoteness from the physical library pose particular challenges for librarians.

What is involved in effectively marketing electronic resources to distance students? How can students be made aware of the wealth of resources available? How can they be helped to achieve proficiency in their use? What initiatives result in increased usage? In seeking to answer these questions, this chapter advocates presenting relevant quality resources which are accessible any time/anywhere. It also affirms offering support at the students' point of need. The value of incorporating into the academic curriculum a requirement to utilize electronic resources is highlighted. The final section examines the effectiveness of a range of standalone approaches which may be used to promote resources.

A PRODUCT WORTH PROMOTING

Marketing means more than simple promotion. It includes offering products and services which are of value to your client group. For an academic library marketing electronic resources, determining the right product mix requires a good understanding of what disciplines are taught in the institution and at what level. It is also important to understand the pedagogical approach taken in various courses, as this influences the level of use of resources. With this information it is possible to determine the best mix of available databases to purchase. Techniques to evaluate products are outside the scope of this discussion, but these should include analysis of ease of use and product trials which allow students to provide feedback. The quality of the interface will affect return visits as shown by surges in use experienced by Academic Press and the American Institute of Physics after they moved to platforms with simplified access.[2] The best product mix will include not only subscription databases, but also free Web resources, electronic course reserves and electronic examination papers. To meet anticipated needs, libraries may require digitization projects or may have to lobby vendors to offer new products.

Efforts to offer good products are relevant to all users, but for remote users the importance of accessibility any time/anywhere is paramount. Distance students are typically workers studying part-time[3] and are time poor. They often need to be able to study late at night or on weekends, times when academic libraries may be closed. While all staff and students benefit from off-campus access to electronic resources, this is essential for distance students. The development of a common sign-on for multiple uses, removing the need for multiple passwords, has greatly assisted distance students. The use of transparent authentication software, such as EZproxy, is equally important. Access is further simplified when students do not have to sign on each time they access another resource during one session.

A message which comes with great clarity from students is that they see accessible resources primarily as full-text resources.[4] Comments made by UNE distance students in 2005 supported this view. Some of the statements made by students include:

- "The most important area to address is to increase the number of online journals available."
- "The number of electronic journals that are subscribed to isn't as big as I'd like, especially as that's the only library service I use, being an overseas student."
- "I don't like to send for photocopies because there is too much delay. Electronic access is preferred . . ."
- "Make more books/papers on the recommended reading lists to each unit available to view in full via the net."
- "My main frustration is the huge expense and time lost due to lack of direct access to relevant full text databases for psychological journals."

Students have a strong preference to use databases which contain a high percentage of full-text materials. Many will prefer to use full-text databases of medium relevance over more relevant citation or abstract only indexes. The marketability of indexes at UNE was significantly enhanced by the addition of SFX links to citation/abstract indexes. This allowed students to connect to full-text articles, where available, from indexes. Fisher and Pride point out that the price of service may include not only fees for service and transportation costs, but also time spent waiting and level of convenience.5 Students are clear that they wish to have online full-text material at a time which suits them. This knowledge can inform us regarding the products and access services we choose to offer and how we promote them.

SUPPORTING SELF-STARTERS

Even if a library does not mount a promotional campaign to distance students, some will come looking for resources to support their study. They may have been instructed in course materials to use the library to enable completion of assignments or may just be independently aware of library services. For these students, effective use of electronic resources will be enhanced by a well-designed Web site which provides advice on how to search competently and makes it easy to discern what to use for particular purposes.

Certain resources are of such self-evident value that minimal publicity will probably result in high usage as long as they are easy to locate on the Web. Past exam papers and electronic reserve full-text articles for individual units of study are examples of products which meet students' information needs. Judith Siess cautions that the real product of the library is not books, journals, reference service, and so on.[6] She states, "A good library provides its customers with *answers* to their questions, with *solutions* to their problems."[7] Usage statistics show that students see full-text resources packaged for a particular unit of study as meeting these criteria.

A unit-specific approach rarely includes all the useful resources for practical and philosophical reasons. Staffing resources would need to be expanded enormously to search multiple resources and prepackage useful items. The upkeep would be huge. University libraries also seek to enhance students' information literacy abilities to equip them for life-long learning. This leaves the library with the challenge to design a Web site which allows students to successfully navigate to resources useful to them. As Cockrell and Jayne have stated,

> On the Web, all resources appear at the click of a mouse button and may look similar. As a result, many users fail to recognize consciously the function of library resources such as the online public access catalog (OPAC), periodical indexes, or a journal collection. It accordingly becomes more difficult but also more necessary to communicate effectively via the library Web site.[8]

There have been a number of studies in this area and these illustrate best practices. The value of providing listings of databases and other resources by discipline is well recognized.[9] A federated search facility is one approach to bringing resources together in discipline groupings. The quality of the search engine will impact students' responses and the likelihood of return visits. What students like can be surprising and does not necessarily match how librarians rate the interface. Interestingly, a study of first-year biology students at the UNE in April 2006 revealed that those who had experienced searching both by using MetaSearch (Ex Libris MetaLib) search boxes and by direct searching, mostly using the CSA interface, had a preference for MetaSearch. This finding appeared surprising to most library reference staff at UNE. Their expectations had been that problems in accessing some relevant databases through MetaSearch federated search software at the time would have led students to rate this resource well below direct searching of native interfaces. However, these findings may not be generally applicable as the students were on-campus enrollees who received group instruction in which they were given search strategies known to lead to available full-text for their assignment. A much larger study in California universities showed only 50.5% of respondents felt the SFX button met their expectations.[10] This finding is possibly more typical of the experience of distance students who have not had their expectations impacted by library staff training or had the benefit of search advice.

Quality help available on Web pages, FAQs and advice to new users, pod casts, guides to using individual databases, and online tutorials will contribute to students' ability to find and use good resources. The effort to produce and maintain these is, however, quite high. The usage of Web-based standalone tutorials is generally low unless they are integrated into a course.[11] At UNE we had thought student interest in guides might not warrant the effort of maintaining them. Interestingly, in 2005, our distance students rated the importance of the clarity of instructions in library guides on how to use databases at 6.14 out of a possible 7. A number offered comments such as:

- "I feel the instructions need to be more basic, i.e., step by step for me as a mature age student."
- "Online tutorials have been helpful."
- "More interactive training systems need to be implemented."

Where such resources are offered, their placement on the Web site is a key consideration. Students seem to have a problem both in realizing that help exists and then in finding it. Terminology is important and studies on what is effective are crucial. A Marshall University Libraries team found "Help," "How do I . . ." and "Ask a Librarian" were preferred terms for students.[12] Headings such as, "How to search for articles" or "Find articles" have been found to resonate with students compared with "databases" or "indexes."[13] Gelman Library, George Washington University, has a large number of subject and database guides, and Web page requests indicate heavy use. Courtois, Higgins, and Kapur attribute usage levels to three factors: a prominent link on the homepage to "Research Guides on Specific Topics"; the fact that most guides cover specific topics or assignment topics, rather than discipline areas; and links for guides under each subject area for article databases.[14]

LINKING INTO THE ACADEMIC CURRICULUM

The priority of students is to pass or excel in their unit of study. This reality means that the authority on how to approach their study resides unquestionably with the lecturer. One of the characteristics of distance education at the UNE has been the offering of voluntary and compulsory residential schools on campus. Several thousand distance students actually attend these schools each year. This provides an opportunity for librarians to meet with distance students both in and outside of classes. For several years, library staff have made use of the opportunity afforded by residential schools to walk around campus talking to students informally, answering questions, telling them about relevant electronic resources and gaining their input. Feedback gained shows that information on resources provided by faculty, combined with a clear requirement to use these resources for assignments, has a major impact on levels of usage. When queried on what databases they use and why, most students refer to a subset of resources of high relevance to them and state that they were told by lecturers to use them. As a case in point, the April residential school regularly attracts a sizeable cohort of psychology students. In 2005, informal feedback from this cohort showed almost all students used online journals and the psycARTICLES database, but they were, in most cases, unaware of psycINFO, the premier index for their field. Faculty were apprised of this situation and pleasingly students at the April 2006 residential school commonly reported being alerted to this major database by their lecturers.

When asked what they thought was the best way to tell them about electronic resources, students agreed that hearing from lecturers would work best. Education students consulted in April 2006 suggested that study guides could include specific information on relevant databases, not the generic information currently included. They also suggested use of online bulletin boards and including advertising with the postal return of marked assignments. A group of Education students believed bulletin boards would have high impact.

Students may also be guided to which resources to use by assessment practices. A 2003 University of Pennsylvania study of Business faculty members found that 72.4% encouraged students to use specific Web sites for assignments and another 10.3% required them to do so.[15] 79.7% insisted on additional sources, but only 12.5% required use of library databases, with a further 41.1% encouraging such use. It should be acknowledged that Web sites provide excellent and valid resources for these students, but greater use of quality subscription databases would be beneficial to many. Dewald found that part-time lecturers were less likely to recommend library databases and she identified a need to work with lecturers to ensure they were aware of the available databases and their value.[16] She also recommended working with them to have students made aware of both good databases and Web sites for particular assignments.

While academics in other disciplines have differing practices in what they require of students, the need to keep lecturers well informed and to use them as marketing agents is, in my view, one key to effective marketing of electronic resources to the majority of students. Faculty will become more enthusiastic to promote electronic resources as they realize the positive benefits in higher-quality student assignments. Galvin reported on collaboration to provide assignment specific pathfinders at Kingsborough Community College in Boston.[17] Economics and English professors, for whom she had created assignment pathfinders, commonly requested the service again as they found student use of scholarly resources increased. Keeping academic staff well informed and committed to promoting library electronic resources is labor intensive, but it will very effectively lead students to the best sources to meet their information needs.

A study of course coordinators done for the University of South Australia Library, seeking reasons for low usage of three specific subscription databases, found that communication about databases by e-mail was problematical as the volume of e-mail creates an information overload.[18] The study also noted a problem with the level of demand for a new product. "Only dramatically better customer benefits very well communicated will change behavior."[19] The recommended solution was a much more personalized information service which is not necessarily feasible or desirable, but the value of face-to-face contact with lecturers was an important point which was also made.

There are many reports in the literature of working with lecturers to embed information literacy skills and knowledge into academic curricula. This entails working collaboratively with faculty to map which abilities in information use and search processes are appropriate for each unit of a course. Course content and assessment strategies support and motivate students as they build these abilities and skills. Strategies include the use of reinforcement through repetition. The level of information literacy required is also gradually increased, starting perhaps at knowing how to find a book in the library catalog and working through to use of citation indexes to track academic debate. While this idea does not immediately appear relevant to the marketing of electronic resources, it is an effective way to do so. From a short-term perspective there may be a conflict between imparting information literacy skills and marketing relevant products. Students generally are not motivated to understand the information-seeking processes and may be discouraged by early requirements to demonstrate high skill levels. Effective marketing may well take advantage of the immediate gratification culture by providing direct links to excellent articles in introductory units. Betty Ladner collaborated with faculty in the School of Nursing at the University of North Carolina at Charlotte to provide research resources outside of the online textbook to undergraduate students.[20] To overcome the frustration which students feel when grappling with the intricacies of online searching, pre-scripted searches were provided to PubMed. PubMed was chosen as it removed the need to sign on multiple times. The aim was to reduce student frustration and allow immersion in the research literature. Students were also given Yahoo search links to enable them to see the difference between scholarly information and much of what is available on the Web. Step-by-step guides to searching for scholarly literature were provided for those interested in learning more. Student feedback was very positive.

Once students appreciate the value of quality scholarly articles, information skills could be gradually enhanced by moving from direct links or pre-scripted searches to independent searching with appropriate help available. By gradually increasing the skill level required, the student will not be discouraged, but will graduate with the ability to continue to seek excellent information sources when the lecturer or librarian is no longer available to prompt them. This approach is only feasible with close cooperation between the library and academic staff.

STANDALONE STRATEGIES

> When serving a distance education population, we cannot passively sit at the reference desk and expect students to come to us . . . our emphasis needs to be on advocating the services we offer and educating our clientele not only in the areas of information literacy but also in the simple knowledge of what resources and services are available.[21]

Strategies to impart awareness of electronic resources mostly fall into three categories: using the contact opportunities afforded by individual students who are seeking help; providing outreach information on the Web site; and proactively delivering information directly to groups of students. The first offers high-quality service to a limited number of students. The last category offers the highest impact with potentially the lowest cost outlay. The impact of providing information on the Web is far-reaching, but also costly.

Responding to Individual Opportunities

Students who contact the library for help are usually open to receiving suggestions on useful electronic sources, whether in direct answer to their immediate question or as an add-on useful information snippet. Even if requested to do so, reference staff are unlikely to consistently promote add-on information either in face-to-face encounters or when responding to phone calls. Time pressures and awareness of student concentration on immediate tasks are restraining factors. Staff are, however, comfortable in promoting databases of immediate relevance to the query.

In the traditional library, distance students were dependent on library reference staff to provide bibliographies of articles and to select books for them when the lecturer had not already given clear recommendations. UNE was proud of its reference and document services in this area and as it became possible for students to access materials electronically, library staff sought strategies to transit students to a more independent approach to locate relevant resources.

Our first strategy was to implement Project Self Help. We continued the traditional approach of sending bibliographies and book loans in response to subject search queries, but where students had requested information via a Web form or e-mail, we sent a series of push e-mails as well. In the first e-mail, we let them know the subject search results were in the mail, informed them that much of what they needed was available online, and let them know we were going to send a series of e-mails to help them build their search skills. We then sent e-mails giving basic information plus Web links for additional information on searching the catalogue, using the Web, and finding and using indexes. We asked for responses (which we rarely received) and after a set period, we rang students to see how they were progressing with the information sent. Feedback on the value of this project was very positive, but it was evident that a good number of students had yet to find time to study the short e-mails. Project Self Help was very time consuming and while it was highly beneficial for students who took advantage of the information sent, it reached only a low number of students. We discontinued the project, but have continued to use the prepared e-mails in response to basic queries on how to find information.

The current strategy in place at UNE still offers highly personalized service. In response to subject queries, distance students are still mailed books where the query is complex and shelf browsing is essential. However, for the bulk of their needs, students receive simple e-mails giving step-by-step strategies to go to and search the catalogue, relevant databases, Google Scholar, and so on. The strategies include key words to use in the search. A final e-mail summarizes what has been sent or e-mailed and suggests additional databases to try if more is needed (see Figures 1-3). Eudora e-mail stationery proved very efficient for this, but any system for canned responses including simple Word files can be used.

This approach has been very well received by most students and has resulted in less repeat users of the service, as the students transfer the approaches gained to other information questions. Sample representative comments made by students are below.

- "I can't thank you enough for the help you have given me. Thanks so much" (third year Industrial Relations subject).
- "Thanks so much. I followed your step by step instructions and was quite successful. It was much better to be taught how to do this myself than be given a list of articles. I have learned how to use a great research tool" (third year Law).

- "... By the way the stuff you have been sending was of great benefit and for my 2 assignments done this semester I have received a Distinction and a High Distinction so I am pleased" (third year Leadership subject).
- "A belated thank you for all your help last week with search strategies. As a consequence of your advice, I managed to locate and/or order everything I need for my assignment. You will no doubt hear from me again–when I find myself in more trouble!!" (first year student).

Each query has quite high staff costs with time taken averaging 44 minutes. However, it offers high-quality service when it is needed and gives students a positive experience either when first finding their way among the multitude of electronic products from which they must choose or when the query is too complex for them at their skill level. This positive guided experience gives students the confidence to use databases independently in the future. It also builds a good relationship with the library, making it easier for them to further seek advice when needed.

Use of co-browsing with a virtual reference service has a similar impact, but presents greater challenges in terms of staff skills and technological barriers. Many of the queries received at UNE are for advanced

FIGURE 1. Start e-mail.

Dear xxx

I have just started your subject search. I will be emailing search strategies and/or references, many of which you will be able to access yourself from home or work.

To access electronic resources from the University Library site you require a UNE username and password. If you do not have one already, register online now by going to *http://www.une.edu.au/library/*
and clicking on 'online registration'.

Online help guides for the journal indexes are at
http://www.une.edu.au/library/elecres/indexguides.htm

Have you looked at the recommended readings in your unit guide? If not, consider requesting loan/copy of those resources that suit your topic.

PRIVACY STATEMENT
The information you provided is used to process your request. The subject search requests are kept on file for one year and are used either as a basis for creating a 'Frequently asked question' topic sheet, or as a reference point if you request additional information. You have the right to access and/or correct any personal information concerning you held by the University, subject to the reasonable convenience of the University.

FIGURE 2. ProQuest strategy e-mail.

Dear xxx

You can access online articles immediately using ProQuest.

The following search works well in ProQuest.
keyword + keyword + keyword

Connect to the Web.
Go to the UNE University Library page at *http://www.unc.edu.au/library/*.
Choose e-resources.

Select ProQuest from the Quick Links on the left.
Enter your UNE username and password when prompted.

Type < xxxxx > in the first search box.
Type < xxxxx > in the second search box.

Mark the box next to 'Full text documents only' if you wish.
Marking the box for 'Scholarly journals, including peer reviewed' will ensure academic sources only.
Click on the search button.

ProQuest will present you with a list of matching articles.
To view an article from the list given, click on the article title or a format icon. Click on Help (top right) for information on the various formats.
To print an article, you must be viewing the article contents as Full Text, Page Impage - PDF or as Text + Graphics.
You can email articles to yourself, either one at a time or by saving a number of articles to a marked list.

If an article is not available in full-text in ProQuest, click on the Find It button to discover its availability through other sources.

Please let me know if you need more help.

units and complex queries. The librarian and the student benefit from staff having time to explore several strategies before suggesting the best one. To do this preparatory work in real time online might be difficult. Nevertheless, both approaches have a place.

Outreach on the Web Site

While it can be frustrating to have students you survey requesting the provision of information that is already available, others will success-fully locate promotional materials provided independently. The value of good Web site design and help materials was covered earlier in the section, "Supporting self-starters." The Web site can also provide infor-mation on new resources on What's New pages, in blogs, or by using changing graphics. To have more impact, this information needs to be highly visible and attractive.

FIGURE 3. Concluding e-mail.

Dear xxx

I have now completed work on your subject search. Let me know if
you need more help with how to find relevant references for this
search. If you wish the University Library to send books and articles to
you, please place your requests through the External Students'
Library Service. See *http://www.une.edu.au/library/external/index.htm* for contact
options.

xx books have been posted to you.

Strategies/search results were sent from the following indexes to identify relevant
journal articles

xxx

Strategies/search results were sent from the following full text databases to locate
relevant articles

xxx

Should you need more information I suggest you go to
http://www.une.edu.au/library/elecres/indexes2.htm
and search in the following indexes/databases

xxx

Information about new products and services must be well presented
to grab the attention of those to whom it is most useful. Take Web of
Science as an example. Just the heading "Web of Science" can easily
turn off the interest of users in the humanities field. Perhaps the announcement would be better headed "Treasure trove for scholars"? The
value of the product should be clear to readers quickly or they will lose
interest. UNE has used large rotating banners in the Web site to advertise products with some success. Usage rose in response to these banners but then leveled off, pointing to the need for continuous change to
attract interest. It may also suggest that the students do not have a high
enough need for the information to increase the rate of return visits.

Direct Delivery

Push e-mails are highly effective. A Psychology student studying a
first year unit confirmed my experience that direct e-mail is high impact
saying, "If I saw an email on services from the library, I would defi-
nitely click on it." For a two-year period, two main approaches were
used at UNE to promote use of electronic resources to a wide audience–
an information sheet about library resources was added to most unit

guides and, at the peak time for research into assignments during the semester, e-mail was sent to distance students outlining basic services and advertising electronic resources. Informal student feedback at the time was that the library communication was excellent. Unfortunately, as many of the resources were, at the time, available only on paper, it also resulted in work overload for the off-campus section of the library due to significantly increased loan and photocopy requests. Bulk e-mails also raise questions with regard to unsolicited e-mails, and legislation and institutional policies must be observed in their use.

Alternatives to using e-mail to promote services include asking students to join a listserv or request RSS feeds of information. UNE Library offers a listserv which is used to promote resources, and spikes in usage can be observed after postings on particular resources. The difficulty is in getting students onto the listserv or RSS feeds in the first place. UNE found again that bulk e-mail was relatively effective, with promotion by lecturers in online units also having impact. Recommendations to join the listserv in booklets mailed out with CD-ROMs of unit material and on the library new-student Web page had some, but very minor impact. This suggests that an eye-catching method which provides a clickable link enhances response because it can be explored easily and immediately. As more and more students access online units, the ideal place for promotion is the portal where they initially login, perhaps using a news blog. Postings on bulletin boards within individual units or across units for a particular discipline may have even greater impact if they can be arranged.

Tom Riedel reported on an exciting approach developed at Regis University with federal grant funding.[22] A Library Notification Module was developed to let distance students know of relevant resources subscribed to by the university. Links to resources already existed in online courses, but Riedel questioned whether students would recognize the value they offered and saw use of push technology as a way to increase the likelihood of students utilizing the resources. The Library Notification Module identified applicants as they moved to student status. These students received an e-mail, or letter if necessary, inviting them to set up computer access, giving library Web site and contact information, and providing directions to subject guides or other course-specific resources. In the first year of operation, resources were hit by about 19% of recipients of an e-mail.[23] The numbers of those who were prompted to set up computer access and visit the Web site were higher. The first contact was very early in the students' first year and may have more impact if sent when students begin focusing on assignment work.

One final approach which perhaps offers greater hope than any other is to piggyback on the popularity of Google. An OCLC report found that 91% of English-speaking college students resident in Australia, Canada, India, Singapore, the United Kingdom and the United States use search engines to seek information.[24] As more subscription databases are searched by Google Scholar and other search engines, and if we can just convince distance students to access the search engine via a library link which includes an authentication string, they will be able to follow an added link to see full-text in resources subscribed to by the library. The potential to help students find relevant resources more easily is immense. A key marketing principle is to provide what clients want. Students want a simple approach to locate full-text online resources. How much easier it will be to market use of Google from the library page to access more full-text, then to succeed in imparting the plethora of concepts we currently try to communicate!

CONCLUSION

To market electronic resources effectively to distance students, we need to ensure that we have relevant, quality full-text online resources which are easily located and accessed. Our promotion should enhance awareness of what is available and its value to users. Advertising must be timed to attract attention when students have a need, and this is primarily when an assignment or other research is occurring. Long-term take up will be greater if initial experiences are positive. It will also be greater where students have a clear need to use the library resources: a need which faculty can create by their assessment strategies.

Effective promotion is likely to be multipronged. Direct e-mail is the most economical way to reach most distance students. Also effective is providing information where students sign into their online units or within their unit information, particularly when it is tailored and highly relevant to their immediate needs. A well-designed Web site is essential. Working in partnership with faculty to embed a staged approach to exposing students to resources is highly recommended. Finally, providing quality advice to students who approach the library for help will build good relationships and encourage return visits to electronic resources.

NOTES

1. Terri Pedersen Summey, "If You Build It, Will They Come? Creating a Marketing Plan for Distance Learning Library Services," *Journal of Library Administration* 41, no. 3/4 (2004).

2 Judy Luther, *White Paper on Electronic Journal Usage Statistics*, 2nd ed. (Washington, D. C.: Council on Library and Information Resources, 2001), 5.

3. Rosemarie Cooper et al., "Remote Library Users–Needs and Expectations," *Library Trends* 47, no. 1 (1998): 51.

4. Lesley Mutinta Moyo and Ellysa Stern Cahoy, "Meeting the Needs of Remote Library Users," *Library Management* 24, no. 6/7 (2003): 288.

5. Patricia H. Fisher and Marseille M. Pride, *Blueprint for Your Library Marketing Plan: A Guide to Help You Survive and Thrive* (Chicago: American Library Association, 2006), 119.

6. Judith A. Siess, *The Visible Librarian: Asserting Your Value with Marketing and Advocacy* (Chicago: American Library Association, 2003), 17.

7. Ibid.

8. Barbara J. Cockrell and Elaine Anderson Jayne, "How Do I Find an Article? Insights from a Web Usability Study," *Journal of Academic Librarianship* 28, no. 3 (2002): 122.

9. Chooi Hon Ho, "Managing the E-Library in a Global Environment: Experiences at Monash University, Australia," *Program: Electronic Library and Information Systems* 38, no. 3 (2004): 170.

10. Jina Choi Wakimoto, David S. Walker, and Katherine S. Dabbour, "The Myths and Realities of SFX in Academic Libraries," *Journal of Academic Librarianship* 32, no. 2 (2006).

11. Annette Skov and Helli Skaerbak, "Fighting an Uphill Battle: Teaching Information Literacy in Danish Institutions of Higher Education," *Library Review* 52, no. 7 (2003): 330.

12. Judith M. Arnold et al., "Does Anyone Need Help out There? Lessons from Designing Online Help," in *Internet Reference Support for Distance Learners*, ed. William Miller and Rita M Pellen (Binghamton, NY: Haworth Information Press, 2005), 121.

13. Ibid, Cockrell and Jayne, "How Do I Find an Article?"

14. Martin P. Courtois, Martha E. Higgins, and Aditya Kapur, "Was This Guide Helpful? Users' Perceptions of Subject Guides," *Reference Services Review* 33, no. 2 (2004).

15. Nancy H. Dewald, "What Do They Tell Their Students? Business Faculty Acceptance of the Web and Library Databases for Student Research," *Journal of Academic Librarianship* 31, no. 3 (2005).

16. Ibid.

17. Jeanne Galvin, "Alternative Strategies for Promoting Information Literacy," *Journal of Academic Librarianship* 31, no. 4 (2005): 353.

18. John Clayton, "Increasing Eproduct Usage: A Report on Attitudes and Behaviors Acting as Barriers to Increased Usage" (Lynton: Effective Marketing Strategy Pty. Ltd., 2000).

19. Ibid, 20.

20. Betty Ladner et al., "Rethinking Online Instruction: From Content Transmission to Cognitive Immersion," *Reference & User Services Quarterly* 43, no. 4 (2004).

21. Marie F. Jones, "Internet Reference Services for Distance Education: Guidelines Comparison and Implementation," in *Internet Reference Support for Distance Learners*, ed. William Miller and Rita M Pellen (Binghamton, NY: Haworth Information Press, 2004), 25.

22. Tom Riedel, "Ahead of the Game: Using Communications Software and Push Technology to Raise Student Awareness of Library Resources," in *The Eleventh Off-Campus Library Services Conference Proceedings*, ed. Patrick B. Mahoney (Binghamton, NY: Haworth Press, Inc., 2005).

23. Ibid, 384.

24. Cathy de Rosa et al. "Perceptions of Libraries and Information Resources: A Report to the OCLC Membership." (Place Published: Dublin, Ohio: OCLC, 2005) http://www.oclc.org/reports/pdfs/Percept_all.pdf.

Word-of-Mouth Marketing Using Peer Tutors

Michelle S. Millet
Clint Chamberlain

INTRODUCTION

Convincing today's technologically savvy undergraduate students to use their college library's resources for their research is a perennial challenge faced by most librarians. In the Age of Google, it seems to be increasingly difficult to get students to consider using anything other than the free Web resources that they are more familiar with, even when better resources are provided by the library. Librarians at Trinity University successfully encourage peer tutors to act as advocates of librarysubscribed electronic resources and to market library resources to incoming first-year students.

In 2001, Trinity University hired a new university librarian who was determined to increase the number of electronic materials offered by the library. Cognizant of the fact that more and more of the library's purchases and subscriptions were in electronic format and that the number of such purchases and subscriptions would soon increase exponentially, the director and other senior librarians at the university advocated for the creation of a position for an electronic resources librarian, which was filled in 2002. It also became apparent that the rapidly changing information environment necessitated the creation of an information literacy program at Trinity, so the following year yet another new librarian arrived, charged with coordinating the library's nascent information literacy program.

THE ENVIRONMENT

Trinity University is a small, private liberal arts college in San Antonio, Texas with approximately 2,500 students. Although Trinity offers some graduate programs, the majority of the students are undergraduates who are comfortable using sources available for free on the Web–but perhaps have not been widely exposed to paid, scholarly resources made available through libraries. As is common with their generation of students, incoming first-year students are especially unaware of the wide variety of resources provided by the library and tend to turn to Internet search engines first in completing research assignments.

Recognizing that students are more likely to prefer the ease with which they can access electronic resources, the librarians at Trinity have made a concerted effort to acquire and provide access to as much electronic content as possible. For example, as of summer 2006, the library at Trinity provided paid access to approximately 180 full-text aggregators, abstract and index databases, or collections of e-journals; the number of e-journals (both publisher-direct and aggregated, as well as open access) made available via the library's Web site had more than doubled since 2002 to over 22,000 titles. Access to these sundry electronic resources comes via a combination of direct subscriptions to ejournals or databases, and participation in a variety of consortial arrangements. Compare this number of electronic titles to the much lower number of print titles held by the Trinity library–around 2,000 titles as of 2006, and perhaps just a few hundred more than that when the number of print subscriptions was at its peak–and it becomes apparent that the library's users have had to adapt to a veritable explosion of electronic content in a relatively short amount of time.

Teaching faculty and librarians alike observed that students were prone to search the free Web first rather than the library's paid content, and we realized that a multitude of approaches were required to help guide students to the appropriate resources. We soon recognized that enlisting the aid of students in the university's peer tutor program could be a key component of spreading the word about our electronic resources.

LITERATURE REVIEW:
PEER TEACHING

Peer-to-peer instruction and guidance have been long-established in the field of education, dating back to the ancient Greeks.[1] It has been the subject of intensive study over the past several decades, although relatively little formal attention has been devoted to its role in higher education until recently.[2] Although a variety of types or models of peer learning have been identified, the type described as peer modeling, in which observers "pattern their thoughts, beliefs, strategies, and actions after those displayed by one or more models" who are their peers,[3] is especially pertinent to the strategy we chose to utilize at Trinity. In spite of the extensive research done on peer-to-peer instruction, guidance, and modeling in the field of education, relatively few studies have been conducted on its role in libraries.[4] Some libraries have established formal programs for peer counseling, tutoring, or instruction that target specific student populations. The University of Michigan's Undergraduate Library, for example, developed a program to train students to assist minority undergraduates,[5] while at Binghamton University, peer advisors were trained to assist undergraduates in the university's education program.[6] More recently, undergraduate peer instructors at the University of Florida received course credit by providing instruction to undergraduates taking courses in anthropology.[7] Undergraduate students have also been hired to provide more generalized training.[8] Students need not be restricted to formalized programs when instructing peers, however; more on-the-fly peer instruction is also possible, as demonstrated at Aston University.[9] Some libraries have also invited students to act as library advocates.[10]

According to Walberg, "PAL [peer-assisted learning] yields gains, not only in knowledge, but in positive attitudes towards the subject matter and intended behavioral skills."[11] This latter effect was especially what we were looking for in a technique to encourage first-year students to use the library's electronic resources; we could provide students with the knowledge of how to use the electronic resources, but their peers could take the instruction further by helping to foster positive attitudes towards the library and all its resources.

THE PLAN FOR OUTREACH

With our newly hired librarians and a revamped Information Commons, the Trinity library tapped every possible group on campus in order to market library services and collections, both print and electronic. The librarians put together a plan to advertise to faculty, facilitated open workshops for students, and also held a day-long "get to know the library" session for campus staff during the quieter summer months.

Tapping into student interests and groups is always a hurdle, especially since the librarians are commonly from different generations than the students. Libraries need to take hold of academic-related issues as often as possible in order to push their own agenda. Marketing library holdings and electronic resources is no different. At Trinity University, we tapped into a wave in academia that hit our campus: the push for academic integrity. As our campus initiated a formal academic integrity policy and an honor council plan (http://www.trinity.edu/departments/academic_affairs/honor_code/index.htm), the library pitched the bibliographic management software product RefWorks to the Office of Academic Affairs as a way to educate students about citation and plagiarism. When Academic Affairs decided to commit half of the funds required to license the software, they also became aware of the need to market the product to students.

As is common at a liberal arts institution, there are no courses required of all students at Trinity University. The faculty pride themselves on their academic freedom, and students relish their ability to choose multiple majors and design a curriculum they truly like, for the most part. This is somewhat of a dilemma for the library because we have no real "captive" audience for all students. We do, however, have a way to indirectly market to first-year students by targeting their peer tutors.

First-years at Trinity are required to take either First-Year Seminar (GNED 1300), usually followed with Writing Workshop (ENGL 1302) or a Humanities seminar that runs throughout the first-year (HUMA 1600). All of these sections are paired with an advanced Trinity student, selected by Academic Affairs and the teaching faculty, called a peer tutor. These peers frequently grade student work and forge a strong bond with the first-years, as well as serve as good academic role models.

PEER TUTOR TRAINING

After Academic Affairs and the Coates Library partnered in the purchase of bibliographic management software and academic integrity education, we were invited to participate in the annual peer tutorial training day. All incoming peer tutors (approximately fifty students) are encouraged to attend the workshop. The day includes time for the peer tutors to get to know one another, sessions on encouraging discussion in a seminar atmosphere, providing proper feedback to first-year students, and an introduction to "the latest and greatest from the library."

Our goals in the session are both obvious and more subversive. We obviously promote RefWorks, while also talking about academic integrity. One cannot, however, demonstrate and teach the nuances of bibliographic management software without also highlighting the best databases for first-year student research and new resources that the library is promoting. The workshop is held every August during the week before all the students begin to return to campus, so it is a great time to reach these students. They are a selective group; the cream of the crop. Their minds are not yet bogged down with coursework and assignments, and they have had to spend a half day listening to teaching faculty lecture at them.

Enter the fun librarians! The Electronic Resources Librarian and the Information Literacy Coordinator are the two librarians who go each year to the program to promote library services. For the past three years, we have talked to the peer tutors about expectations of library use (or non-use) of first-years, their research capabilities, and promote good, general academic resources like EBSCO's *Academic Search Premier*. We also, of course, promote our bibliographic management software and encourage the peer tutors to create accounts for themselves and promote the product among the first-years. The final goal is to introduce them to a new resource or library feature; this part of our agenda changes every year, depending on what new resources we have added. In the past, we have shown them how to access the OpenURL resolver. We have also highlighted a new database, such as *American Civil War: Letters and Diaries,* to highlight primary source content resources.

During the fall 2005 workshop, we also introduced our new tutorials, created by an instruction librarian, that demonstrate how to import or export citations from each of the different vendor databases to which the library subscribes. The students thought this was a great new feature, since they ran into problems because each vendor directly exports citations to the software in a different manner. At the end of the workshop, each student is also provided with a basic handout that includes instructions on creating a RefWorks account and tips for working with first-year students and research tips (see Appendices 1 and 2).

MEASURING SUCCESS

So far, each year the peer tutors are bowled over by the bibliographic management software and they are always excited to find out about the products we are promoting. Last year, for the first time a number of peer tutors had created RefWorks accounts for themselves prior to the start of the fall 2005 semester. In the previous year, there were no students in the room with existing accounts.

Statistically speaking, our campus does well in promoting RefWorks and we have a high percentage of students who use the software. Examining our current year's statistics can lead to a couple of conclusions. For this past year, the two months when we had the greatest number of new users were September and October 2005, with 124 and 115 new users respectively. This leads us to believe that most of the new user accounts are created by first-years. While we do not have direct evidence to support that assertion, first-year students are most likely to be in the library during those months for information literacy instruction with their First-Year Seminars, using the Writing Center (also located in the library), and working closely with their peer tutors. Also, when new users sign up for a RefWorks account, they are asked to list a user type and focus area. Out of 1098 total undergraduate accounts created from 2004-2006, 312, over one-third of the accounts, noted "other" as their focus area–more than any other area–which leads us to believe that first-years were the ones creating those accounts, as sophomores and up would probably have a better idea of their major.

The other electronic resource that we market and promote heavily with our first-year peer tutors is EBSCO's *Academic Search Premier* database. As librarians, we choose to encourage first-year students to utilize this database in their early research for a variety of reasons. First, it provides them with a great likelihood for success. One reason that students like to use Internet search engines is because they return a lot of hits. Without evaluating the quality of those results, students visualize success in terms of the number of results returned. *Academic Search Premier* also contains both scholarly and popular content and is thus a fertile ground for exploring the difference between the two types of materials and allowing students to begin evaluating the quality of the information early in their college careers.

As Table 1 demonstrates, our usage statistics for *Academic Search Premier* have grown exponentially. While our overall information literacy instruction sessions have also increased over 100% since 2001, most of the usage during September and October can be attributed to First-Year Seminar information literacy instruction sessions and use by first-year students. There is no doubt in our minds that working with the peer tutors has increased the visibility of good, scholarly electronic resources and these two resources in particular.

TABLE 1. Usage Statistics for Academic Search Premier Database

Academic Year	September	October
2001/02	944	1907
2002/03	1883	3057
2003/04	2016	5699
2004/05	4862	7478
2005/06	5183	9315

Source: Trinity University, Reference Department Usage Statistics, 2006. Used with permission.

Our last success in working with the peer tutors has been that these upper division students now see the library, and librarians, as a helpful resource for themselves and the classes. Three peer tutors brought their classes in for information literacy instruction on their own accord last year because they sensed the students needed the guidance–where the teaching faculty may not have seen the need. Those three classes are small in comparison with the overall number of sessions taught, but they are a tremendous victory when one thinks that forty-five first-year students had an introduction to research that they would not have had otherwise.

FUTURE PLANS FOR MARKETING

Our library continues to promote our resources in a variety of ways. In the fall of 2006, we will again work to put together a series of sessions promoting resources directly to faculty. It is a strong belief of the librarians at Trinity University that faculty must be made aware of resources before they will promote them through assignment design.

Beginning with the graduating class of 2008, every senior at Trinity University will have to undertake a seminar-type class and project such as a senior thesis, capstone project, or other major project, providing students with an outlet to show what they have learned in four years. In the library, we expect that this will cause demand for resources and instruction to rise and are putting together a plan to offer open workshops for popular majors and workshops that again focus on bibliographic management software and citation methods.

CONCLUSIONS

While it certainly takes a lot of work to plan for and time to attend campus workshops and reach out to various student groups, it never hurts to raise the visibility of librarians and market our resources. While we all continue to pour the majority of our budgets into electronic resources, we must allocate the staff and resources to ensure that our communities remain aware of the worthwhile resources we provide to our patrons.

Much of the literature in marketing suggests that word-of-mouth is an important factor in how consumers make decisions, and there is also evidence that advertising a product or service may be a useful means of encouraging word-of-mouth "buzz."[12] It has been recognized that to generate word-of-mouth "buzz," "the key . . . is to locate the opinion leaders for your particular product or service and find a way of getting them talking about your product or service."[13] Peer tutors are one of the obvious groups of opinion leaders at Trinity University, especially in regards to first-year students. Marketing the library's services and resources directly to peer tutors has been an effective means of creating word-of-mouth promotion of services and resources to the first-years.

We believe that working with the peer tutors has provided a great outlet to promote electronic resources and we are confident after reviewing qualitative and quantitative data of electronic resource usage that working with these advanced students has promoted our resources to the first-year population. In a liberal arts environment, when we have no set way of reaching incoming students, this time with their peer tutors has proven invaluable.

NOTES

1. Lilya Wagner, *Peer Teaching: Historical Perspectives* (Westport, CT: Greenwood Press, 2002).

2. Shirley Hill, Brian Gay, and Keith Topping, "Peer-Assisted Learning Beyond School," in *Peer-Assisted Learning*, ed. Keith J. Topping. (Mahwah, NJ: Lawrence Erlbaum Associates, Inc., 1998), 291-311.

3. Dale H. Schunk, "Peer Modeling," in *Peer-Assisted Learning*, eds. Keith J. Topping and Stewart W. Ehly. (Mahwah, NJ: Lawrence Erlbaum Associates, Inc., 1998), 185-202.

4. Jana Ronan and Mimi Pappas, "Library Instruction is a Two-Way Street: Students Receiving Course Credit for Peer Teaching at the University of Florida," *Education Libraries* 25, no. 1 (Summer 2001): 19-24.

5. Barbara MacAdam and Darlene P. Nichols, "Peer Information Counseling: An Academic Library Program for Minority Students," *Journal of Academic Librarianship* 15, no.4 (September 1989): 204-209; Barbara MacAdam and Darlene P. Nichols, "Peer Information Counseling at the University of Michigan Undergraduate Library," *Journal of Academic Librarianship* 14, no. 2 (May 1988): 80-81.

6. Prue Stelling, "Student to Student: Training Peer Advisors to Provide BI at Binghamton University Library for a Required Course in the School of Education and Human Development," *Research Strategies* 14 (Winter 1996): 50-55.

7. Ronan and Pappas, "Library Instruction is a Two-Way Street," 19-24.

8. Susan Deese-Roberts and Kathleen Keating, "Integrating a Library Strategies Peer Tutoring Program at the University of New Mexico," *Research Strategies* 17 no. 2/3 (2001): 223-229; Karin de Jager, "Navigators and Guides: The Value of Peer Assistance in Student Use of Electronic Library Facilities," *VINE: The Journal of Information & Knowledge Management Systems* 34, no. 3 (2004): 99-106.

9. Amanda Poulton, "Peer Teaching: An Aston Experiment," *SCONUL Newsletter* 31 (Spring 2004): 32-34.

10. Amy Deuink and Marianne Seller, "Students as Library Advocates: The Library Student Advisory Board at Pennsylvania State-Schuylkill," *College & Research Libraries News* 67, no. 1 (January 2006): 18-21.

11. Walberg, Herbert J. "Foreword," in *Peer-Assisted Learning*, eds. Keith J. Topping and Stewart W. Ehly (Mahwah, NJ: Lawrence Erlbaum Associates, Inc., 1998), ix-xii.

12. Barry L. Bayus, "Word of Mouth: The Indirect Effects of Marketing Efforts," *Journal of Advertising Research* 25, no. 3 (1985): 31-39.

13. Chip Walker, "Word of Mouth," *American Demographics* 17, no. 7 (1998): 38-44.

APPENDIX 1
RefWorks Handout 2005-2006

RefWorks
Web-Based Bibliographic Management Service

With RefWorks, you can:

- **create**, **organize**, and **annotate** your own database of bibliographic references—no more 3x5 notecards!
- **import references** from the online catalog or from many of the library's databases
- **automatically format** your bibliographies to conform to a variety of citation styles, including APA, MLA, and the Chicago Manual of Style
- **insert properly formatted citations** into your papers using the Write-and-Cite plug-in for PC or the One Line/Cite View feature for Mac

Get started:

1. **Access** RefWorks from the library's homepage. Go to the "Learn how to . . ." section, under "Cite Sources / Use RefWorks."
2. **Set up** an account. Click on "Sign up for an individual account" and enter your user information. Once your account is established, you can log in and use RefWorks from any computer with an internet connection.
3. **Create** a database of references by automatically importing data from the online catalog or online databases, or by typing references in manually.
4. **Organize** your references by sorting them into folders, editing records to include only information you want, annotating entries, or providing your own descriptors that will enable you to find related records quickly and **easily**.
5. Format your paper and bibliography using the Write-N-Cite plug-in for PC or One Line/Cite View for Mac. Simply find where you want to cite a reference in your paper and insert the RefWorks ID number that reference is assigned in your database. RefWorks will format your citations, create footnotes if necessary, and create a formatted bibliography.

* * *

Need help? Contact the Help Desk (x7213) or use the extensive online help provided by RefWorks, including a helpful online tutorial and quick-start guide.

APPENDIX 2
Tips on Working with First-Year Students

First-Year Students and Library Research

1. Start with Easier Resources
(They Don't Know as Much as You!)
- Library Catalog
- Academic Search Premier

2. Encourage Them to Ask Questions
- Library Help Desk
- Research Consultation Request Online!

3. Go With Them to See a Librarian or Find the Writing Center!

A Three-Step Approach to Marketing Electronic Resources at Brock University

Shelley L. Woods

INTRODUCTION

To effectively market electronic resources, librarians should have a marketing plan that includes knowing the community they serve, promoting the library's resources, and evaluating user satisfaction with the resources. This chapter will describe activities in these three areas at the James A. Gibson Library and Faculty of Education Information Resource Center, Brock University, St. Catharines, Ontario.

MISSION, GOALS AND INITIATIVES

Marketing a library's electronic resources requires an annual marketing plan. A survey conducted by Shiva Kanaujia of R&D Library and Information Centers in India revealed that librarians had positive attitudes toward marketing in libraries, but failed to adopt a coherent marketing plan. Kanaujia suggests that a library's marketing plan should address "operating context, objectives of the year, the four Ps [products and services, place, pricing and promotion], staff training and budget requirements."[1] Stated differently, Ann Wolpert writes, "a marketing strategy must include product planning, technical assistance and communications."[2] Product planning is the "development of product packages." Technical assistance is "helping students access and manipulate the library's resources," and communications is "advertising the library and its services and receiving feedback." A good marketing plan should be based on the library's mission statement, strategic goals and initiatives. The Gibson Library's mission is "to provide access to information resources, services and facilities of the highest possible quality in support of the teaching, learning and research programs of the Brock University community." Based on the mission statement, the library's 2006-2009 Strategic Plan includes six strategic objectives. The objectives are:

- Develop strong Library collections.
- Strengthen the Library's educational role.
- Improve Library facilities to create inviting venues conducive to learning.

- Utilize technology to enhance teaching, learning and research.
- Promote the Library through effective communication strategies.
- Foster a shared commitment to the Library's goals by creating an organizational culture of learning.[3]

Three of the library's six strategic objectives include one or more initiatives related to building and marketing the electronic resources collection. Use of technology will "provide seamless access to information resources," and collection development will have "an emphasis on digital resources that are available 24/7." The Library will "promote and strengthen awareness of its services and resources within the Brock community and beyond to create a shared and informed understanding of its role as a partner in teaching, learning and research, and to develop a strong base of donor support."

KNOWING THE COMMUNITY

To understand the community, librarians at Brock University have surveyed the distinct user groups (faculty, students, alumni) at various points in time. "One would think that academic and special libraries would know precisely who their user community is and be able to target their marketing much more easily than a public library. Theoretically this is true. Academic librarians know that their community consists of faculty, students and administrative staff, but their image of these potential library customers may be inaccurate or outdated."[4]

Brock has a diverse student body of over 17,000 students who study full- and part-time at the undergraduate and graduate levels on campus and at a distance. Distance students are a growing segment of the user population with distinct needs. They are heavy users of the library's electronic resources. Their most basic needs are access to full-text resources, a supportive librarian, and helpful documentation–all available online. "System up/down time, database relevancy (especially in fulltext), document delivery response times, telephone support (including toll free calls), online finding aids and coaching tools, and course-specific Web-based services and products may be more meaningful to students learning at a distance than is the number of monographs added to the collections."[5]

SURVEYS

Surveys are one type of assessment instrument that allow librarians to collect specific and current data based on participants' responses to carefully worded questions. "Most library surveys are snapshots of a situation at one particular point in time."[6]

The Communication/Marketing Implementation Working Group conducted a survey written by Associate University Librarian–Services Debbie Kalvee in February and March 2005 to "gather information about how Brock University faculty members use the Library, how the Library is currently meeting their needs, and how to best communicate with them." One question asked faculty members how "they hear about the Library's news and how they would like to." Faculty members were each permitted three responses to the question. Most faculty members (49.5% of replies) learned about the library's news via e-mails sent by their departmental library subject specialist. Forty-eight and a half percent of responses were for the library's Web site, 39.2% for the *Brock News* newsletter, 38.1% for library staff, 35.1% for printed newsletters, 25.8% for other faculty or staff members and 13.4% for posters. Faculty members preferred reading *Library News* through e-mail and the library Web site. Sixty-six percent of faculty members responded positively to the suggestion of a regular library newsletter to be circulated by e-mail.[7] The responses of faculty members to the survey led to increased library promotions by subject specialists through regular e-mail newsletters and on the library Web site.

The Library Advisory Committee (LAC) of the Faculty of Education Information Resource Center (IRC) wrote a survey for administration to 651 Associate teachers in fall 2006. The purpose of the survey is to discover who is using or is not using the center's resources and services and why, to measure their level of satisfaction or dissatisfaction, and to understand their needs. It asks participants for information relating to demographics, and their awareness, usage and satisfaction with library resources, services and staff. There are questions that deal specifically with identifying the library's competition and participants' reasons for not using the library as well as a section for general comments. Results of the survey will uncover the IRC's Strengths, Weaknesses, Opportunities and Threats (SWOT). Similar to a SWOT analysis, the data gathered pertaining to internal and external factors will be valuable in planning for the center's future.

PROMOTING LIBRARY RESOURCES

Marketing can be defined as "the process of creating a product, then planning and carrying out the pricing, promotion, and placement of that product by stimulating buying exchanges in which both buyer and seller profit in some way."[8] While the focus for libraries is not about pricing and buying exchanges, but rather about product promotion (advertising) and placement, the phrase "in which both parties profit" is true. "The key to success in the new digital world is to cultivate customer relations, to turn the client, the user, the customer into a partner, in a mutually beneficial relationship."[9] The library would not exist without its user base, and the library provides valuable resources and services to those people in return.

It is strongly suggested that librarians develop a plan to market their resources and services. "Importantly, marketing is increasingly commonplace in nonprofit organizations such as libraries, art museums, charities, and political parties. Whatever the nature of the product or service, good marketing helps."[10] A marketing plan should guide the direction of the library's promotion efforts.

A Library Promotion Working Group formed at Brock wrote a Marketing and Communication Plan for the library in 2003. This document set out a time frame, goal, quantifiable objectives, positioning statement, key message, target audiences, strategies, evaluations and considerations. While the Marketing and Communication Plan did not focus solely on electronic resources, it did address that part of the collection.

Marketing strategies proposed by the group include:

- Establishing an annual marketing/communications budget, calendar and working group.
- Developing a graphic identity or to brand all promotional materials.
- Promoting the library's resources on the Web site and through WebCT.
- Using the message "24/7 access @ your library" in promotional materials such as door hangers and mouse pads.
- Creating posters and brochures communicating the themes of currency and abundance of materials–available in electronic and other formats.
- Introducing "Library News" section to the Web site and made available via e-mail.[11]

Usage statistics were kept to aid in evaluation and assessment of the plan. An analysis of the data showed increased database hits and library Web site and catalog hits (including eBook titles).

CONSORTIUM

Most of Gibson Library's electronic resources are purchased through the Ontario Council of University Libraries (OCUL), an Ontario-wide consortium with twenty member libraries. OCUL manages 118 database licenses to databases that are accessible either in the member library, or remotely with a PIN through a portal called Scholars Portal. The goal of "Scholars Portal is to provide access to scholarly electronic resources through a set of tools which allows the networked scholar to search, save and integrate these resources with their teaching and research to foster greater learning opportunities."[12] Scholars can cross-search databases and full-text journal collections and export citations into RefWorks software to compile bibliographies. In addition, Net Library eBooks are purchased by the consortium and listed in the library catalog.

Participation in the consortium enables the Gibson Library to acquire significantly more resources than it could purchase independently. Memberships in consortiums are becoming increasingly advantageous to libraries. "As more colleges and universities engage in remote teaching and learning through the Internet, they will expect their own libraries to support these offerings, probably without any expansion in budgets."[13] Consortial spending at the national level in Canada is similarly focused on acquiring electronic resources. In August 2005, the Canadian Association of Research Libraries announced that for the first time, spending on electronic journals surpassed spending on print serials.[14]

INSTRUCTION

Instructional sessions are used at the Gibson Library to promote electronic resources. Sessions are advertised on the library Web site, on posters and in e-mails to faculty and students.

During Orientation Week the library offers tours and introductory sessions called Smart Start Library to acquaint incoming students with the library's services and collections (including online databases and resources available via the Web site). Students are asked to complete a short printed questionnaire following the session to help the library measure the effectiveness of instructional sessions. The questionnaire also provides insights on the influence of orientation leaders in persuading students to participate in the instructional class. Of the two hundred and eighty participants who completed questionnaires in September 2005, 87% of the respondents replied either "agree" or "strongly agree" in response to the comment "Orientation leaders influenced my decision to attend." These numbers demonstrate the value of word-of-mouth advertising. The number of students who credited their orientation leader with affecting their decision to attend the library session was double the number of students who did not.

Student comments indicated that they valued learning how to use the library's databases, Web site and catalog by accessing these resources from a laptop and wireless connection during the session. Sample responses to the open-ended question "What was the best thing about this session?" included:

"Learning how to use the online library resources."
"Informing me about using the library online."
"Learning about newspaper databases."
"Ability to use library resources from home."

Later in the semester students may receive specialized instruction during class time if it is arranged by a faculty member, or outside of class time, by completing an "Order a Workshop" form from the library's Web site (see Figure 1). Students who register through the "Order a Workshop" form may register with their classmates or friends and meet with the librarian at a mutually agreed upon time. These instructional sessions, because they are personalized, have a good response rate with fewer students registering for the session but failing to attend.

The goals of instructional sessions are to promote the library's resources as scholarly and reliable, highlight special features of the resources, teach literacy skills, and present the library as a welcoming place. Students are given a paper questionnaire to complete at the end of the session. In addition to asking for their year of study, satisfaction with the format, content and relevance of the session and perceived learning, one of the questions is "How did you learn about this workshop?"

FIGURE 1. Web Site Advertisement for RefWorks

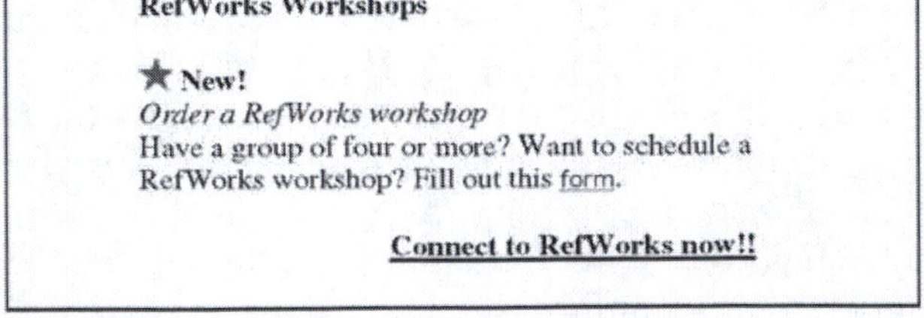

RefWorks Workshops

★ **New!**
Order a RefWorks workshop
Have a group of four or more? Want to schedule a
RefWorks workshop? Fill out this form.

Connect to RefWorks now!!

Fourteen Info Skills Plus workshops covering online searching basics, advanced searching, and citing and evaluating sources were offered in fall 2005, attracting 129 participants. Of the total number of participants, 106 completed the questionnaire. Forty people (37.7% of respondents) saw the workshop advertised on the library's Web site. Twenty-six people (25% of respondents) knew about the sessions from their professors or because it was announced in class. Seventeen people (16% of respondents) had attended an earlier session and were repeat participants. Library signs and career services (who offer workshops in conjunction with the library) recruited nine people each. Other referrals came from friends of the participants (two people), Reference Staff (two people), and a teaching assistant (one person). Based on these numbers, the most effective means of advertising training sessions for online searching, and citing and evaluating at Brock is on the Library Web site. The Gibson Library homepage receives approximately 150,000 hits a month, further proving its effective use as a marketing tool. Word-of-mouth was also an effective way to advertise library instruction sessions, as it was for Smart Start Library.

LIBRARY WEB SITE AS PROMOTIONAL TOOL

A library's Web site is both a product in the sense that it is produced by or for library staff, and an advertisement that promotes the library's resources and services. As access to new databases is added, they are spotlighted on the Gibson Library's Web site both in the Library News section and displayed visually with a rotating, clickable icon (see Figures 2 and 3).

FIGURE 2. Web Site Advertisement for Access to New Databases

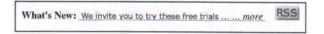

FIGURE 3. Web Site Announcement for ARTstor Database

Whenever several new electronic resources become available simultaneously, as is possible through consortial agreements, increased advertising is done. Besides making faculty aware of the new resources through conversation, e-mail, and departmental newsletters, a press release (see Appendix A) is printed in *Brock News*, a newsletter that is circulated to university faculty and staff, and posted on the library's Web site. Ideas for future publications include articles about how students and faculty are using the new resources, will be printed in other university and external newspapers. The Brock University homepage featured a photograph for one week of a student, faculty member, and librarian accessing one of the new databases from a library laptop.

Another page on the Web site lists new databases and includes a short description of content and years of coverage; this information can be found in Appendix B. In an effort to solicit feedback, and to take advantage of the interactive nature of the online access, the page also includes a "Tell us what you think of our new resources!" link for user comments. The Associate University Librarian-Collection Resources is planning an event in the library's e-classroom to showcase the new electronic resources and the changing academic library.

De Saez writes about library marketing in the digital age, saying that librarians need to develop "mutually beneficial relationships" with users.[15] With regard to the World Wide Web, De Saez believes that libraries can learn from company Web sites and features that companies use to develop loyalty in their customers. Such features include personalized greetings and e-mails, and the opportunity for two-way communication that develops a relationship with the customer and nurtures the feeling of being valued. In libraries, "readers and users logging into the system can be addressed by name and encouraged to return by specifically targeted information of interest to them: warned that loan materials are about to expire, new items are in stock, new online services available in their subject area, and new legislation enacted relevant to their range of products."[16]

E-MAIL

Elsevier warns to "avoid generic e-mail alerts to a wide audience in favor of tailored e-mail messages."[17] Library users, including faculty and staff, do not want to receive daily e-mails from their well-meaning librarian. E-mail messages should be sent to a specific person or group of people when there is relevant information to exchange, not every time that the library acquires a new resource. Librarians may use e-mail to send users information and links that are pertinent to that person's research area. Such personalized and meaningful correspondence will be better received than mass mailings. Sending out targeted e-mail messages increases the chance that the message will be read, because it is sent directly to the user, rather than waiting for the user to discover the information on his or her own.

EVALUATION

Evaluation of library resources and services needs to move beyond usage statistics, although these are important pieces of information. "Inevitably, the development of metrics and standards for the measurement of the digital library has lagged behind the development of the digital library itself."[18]

There are currently 57 faculty and 1,887.3 full time equivalent students, 232.2 who are enrolled at the graduate level in Brock University's Faculty of Education. Figure 4 shows education-related database usage for the months of July 2005-September 2006.

FIGURE 4. Database Usage (July 2005-September 2006)

Database	Use: July 2005-Sept.2006
Academic Search Premier	6737
ERIC	3116
Education: a Sage Full-Text Collection	2044
CBCA Complete	1163
Educational Administration Abstracts	408
Psychology: a Sage Full-Text Collection	375
Scholars Portal E-Journals	562
PsycINFO	326
LLBA (Linguistics and Language Behavior Abstracts)	222
Ingenta	191
Sociological Abstracts	193
PsycCRITIQUES	151
Web of Science	149
RefWorks	157

In April 2006 a new subject search feature was added to Scholar's Portal. Researchers can select subject searching from the Scholar's Portal interface. They can select Education as a subject and cross-search ERIC, Education: a Sage Full-Text Collection and Educational Administration Abstracts. Subject searching is explained on the subject specialist's Library Research in Education guide available in PDF on the Library Web site. This new automatic cross-search feature is listed first on the Library Research in Education guide, and it received relatively high use over the summer session, with 748 searches between April and September.

The Database page (which lists databases by subject area) is accessed between 5,000 and 10,000 times a month, more often than the Reference page (which lists online resources such as other university sites and government sites by topic and is accessed between 200 and 700 times a month). The positioning of advertising, on the page and on the Web site, will impact the effect that the advertising has on library users.

In addition to the databases, Brock University students currently have access to 7,135 Net Library non-fiction and fiction eBook titles, 3,400 of which are publicly accessible titles. The Gibson Library purchased 4,000 eBooks in the summer of 2004 and added to the collection in the summer of 2005. Between the summer of 2004 and December 2006 eBooks were used 5,397 times.

The library has not widely advertised its eBook collection beyond including it in the News section of the Web site, which is also available as automatic e-mail updates through RSS (news syndication software). Subject specialists may choose to highlight new collections such as the eBook collection in their newsletters which are either sent in print or electronically, and may be posted as a PDF to their Web page. The Business and Economics Librarian, whose segment of the population accessed the library's eBooks most often (see Figure 5), included the new eBook collection in the September 2004 newsletter.

Not surprisingly, eBook use at Brock also relates to the focus of the collection and user demographics. The programs with the greater number of students were also the subjects with higher eBook use. Based on numbers of undergraduate full-time equivalency numbers, the largest seven programs at Brock University map to the highest e-Books usage. The other subject areas receiving high eBook use are also larger to medium-sized programs of study at Brock. The eBook user statistics show the importance of knowing the user group and their needs, information that should guide librarians not only in marketing activities, but also in planning for the library collection and services. "Measurement of digi-

FIGURE 5. eBook Use According to Discipline

Discipline	Number of Uses	Percentage of Use
Business, Economics and Management	1346	20.4%
General Social Sciences	993	15%
Medicine	777	11.8%
Literature	584	8.8%
Computer Science	481	7.3%
World and General History	292	4.4%
Psychology	265	4.0%
Philosophy	258	3.9%
Education	220	3.3%
Language and Linguistics	181	2.7%

tal library services has a valuable role to play in supporting day-to-day library management, service development, reporting, marketing and advocacy."[19]

Assessment or evaluation is strongest when it combines quantitative (numerical and structured), and qualitative (more open-ended and comment-based) measures. Each year in March, librarians at the Gibson Library poll the on-campus users by circulating a printed form with three straightforward yes-or-no questions that relate to their satisfaction with the library collection and staff. "Did you find what you needed?" is one of the questions. It also asks for suggestions on how to improve upon the library's existing collection and services. Patrons who answer the questions may anonymously submit the form in one of several boxes strategically placed throughout the library. An interesting by-product of the survey is that student feedback from questionnaires can be turned into marketing slogans. As a general comment after a Ref Works and Write and Cite (citation management software) workshop, a student wrote "Ref Works = excellent."

CONCLUSION

Marketing is a process, the basic principles of which (products and services, place, pricing and promotion), may be applied to marketing electronic resources in libraries. Five key suggestions for academic libraries are listed below:

- Develop and maintain an up-to-date marketing plan that is aligned with the library's mission and goals. Solicit input from staff and management.
- Research the user and potential user to understand their needs and enter into a reciprocal relationship with them. A survey is one way to understand user needs. Focus groups, interviews and observation are others. Research data can be used to improve or add library services.
- Assess the competition and learn what contributes to their success.
- Use word-of-mouth, e-mail, press releases, the library Web site, special events, library instruction, printed advertisements and special events to promote electronic resources. A multi-faceted approach to advertising is the most effective way to ensure your message is heard.

Information needs are changing at Brock with increasing numbers of graduate-level programs and courses, and new faculty members and students. By surveying library users the Gibson Library is able to tailor its instructional sessions to support specific course requirements. Brock has successfully compiled survey data to learn what databases are most desired by faculty members, and how faculty, staff, and students prefer receiving library updates. Valuable information gathered from regularly conducting surveys guides the development of e-resources collections at Brock and influences the Gibson Library's approaches to marketing the collection.

NOTES

1. Shiva Kanaujia, "Marketing of Information Products and Services in Indian R& D Library and Information Centres." *Library Management* 25, no. 8/9 (2004): 356.

2. Ann Wolpert, "Services to Remote Users: Marketing the Library's Role," *Library Trends* 47, no. 1 (Summer 1998), Academic Search Premier Database, EBSCOhost (accessed January 25, 2006).

3. James A. Gibson Library, "Strategic Plan" [Strategic Objectives], April 2006, http://www.brocku.ca/library/about/typlan.pdf (accessed September 26, 2006).

4. Jeannette A. Woodward, *Creating the Customer-Driven Library: Building on the Bookstore Model* (Chicago: American Library Association, 2005), 135-136.

5. Wolpert, "Services to Remote Users."

6. Peter Hernon, and Ellen Altman, *Assessing Service Quality: Satisfying the Expectations of Library Customers* (Chicago: American Library Association, 1998), 152.

7. Brock University James A. Gibson Library, "Results of the James A. Gibson Library Survey of Faculty 2005," http://www.brocku.ca/library/facsurvey.htm (accessed June 16, 2005).

8. Sarah White, *The Complete Idiot's Guide to Marketing Basics* (New York, NY: Alpha Books, 1997), 4.

9. Eileen Elliott De Sáez, *Marketing Concepts for Libraries and Information Services.* 2nd ed. (London: Facet Publishing, 2002), 141.

10. Rita W. Moss and Diane Wheeler Strauss, *Strauss's Handbook of Business Information: A Guide for Librarians, Students, and Researchers.* 2nd ed. (Westport, CT: Libraries Unlimited, 2004), 158.

11. James A. Gibson Library Promotion Working Group, "*Final Report* 2003," IRIS Intranet, Brock University.

12. Ontario Council of University Libraries [Home Page], http://www.ocul.on.ca/ (accessed April 5, 2006).

13. Peter Hernon, and John R. Whitman, *Delivering Satisfaction and Service Quality: A Customer-Based Approach for Libraries* (Chicago: American Library Association, 2001), 163.

14. Canadian Association of Research Libraries "Research Library Spending on Electronic Serials Surpasses Print Serials for the First Time," http://www.carl-abrc.ca/ projects/statistics/pdf/media%20release-2005-e.pdf (accessed February 21, 2005).

15. De Sáez, *Marketing Concepts*, 141.

16. De Sáez, *Marketing Concepts*, 144.

17. Elsevier, 15 Ways to Promote Effective Use of Online Resources, Library Connect 2003, http://www.elsevier.com/framework_librarians/LibraryConnect/lcpamphlet1. pdf (accessed March 27, 2006).

18. Jane Barton, "Measurement, Management and the Digital Library." *Library Review* 53, no. 3 (2004): 138.

19. Barton, "Measurement," 138.

APPENDIX A
Press Release

LIBRARY LEAPS INTO THE FUTURE BY PROVIDING DIGITAL ACCESS TO THE PAST

The James A. Gibson Library has taken a significant step forward by acquiring access to hundreds of thousands of digital books (*Early English Books Online* and *Eighteenth Century Collections Online*), more than 400,000 art images (*ARTstor*), tens of thousands of classical recordings delivered by streaming audio (*Classical Music Library* and *Naxos Music Library*), and countless primary texts, plays and film scripts (*Alexander Street Press Collection*). The Library has also acquired the digital archive of the *Globe and Mail*, a rich historical resource that includes every news story, photograph, advertisement, and classified ad published by the newspaper since its inception in 1844. The availability of this critical mass of content via the Internet represents a dramatic change in the way students and researchers alike can access these unique resources at any hour from virtually any location. Advances in technology have also meant that in addition to text files, scholars will have timely access to high quality image and sound files.

According to Dr. John Sainsbury, Director of the Humanities Research Institute, these new resources "will revolutionize the ways that we organize student assignments in History and English and perhaps in other disciplines as well. Now we have the option of basing assignments on hitherto unattainable primary sources, thus providing a greater intellectual challenge for students, while minimizing the possibilities of plagiarism."

These major acquisitions also represent a significant asset to Brock in its transition to comprehensive university status. According to Dr. John Lye, Chair of English Languages and Literature, *"Early English Books Online* is now considered a necessary and expected research tool in English Studies, and with our acquisition of this resource we will be able to attract faculty members and graduate students with serious research interests in the Early Modern period."

Many of these resources have been acquired through the Library's participation in the Electronic Content Expansion Project of the Canadian Research Knowledge Network (CRKN). The Project's goal was to secure a critical mass of social sciences and humanities scholarly content in digital formats and to add incrementally to the science/technology/health scholarly content already licensed by CRKN on behalf of university libraries.

For more information on any of these resources, please consult the Library's web site at http://www.brocku.ca/library or contact Pamela Jacobs at pamela.jacobs@brocku.ca or by telephone at ext. 3961.

February 22, 2006

APPENDIX B
Gibson Library Website

New Online Resources for 2006

The James A Gibson Library is pleased to announce the availability of the following new electronic resources for 2006.
For more details, read our PRESS RELEASE (PDF format).

• ARTstor Digital Library	• Early English Books Online (EEBO)
• Alexander Street Press	• Eighteenth Century Collections Online (ECCO)
• Classical Music Library	• Literature Online (LION)
• Globe and Mail: Canada's Heritage from 1844	• NAXOS Music Library
• Oxford Dictionary of National Biography	• Wharton Research Database Service (WRDS)

For access, please click on the links below.
Tell us what you think of our new resources!

A R T S T O R

The *ARTstor Digital Library* is a repository of hundreds of thousands of digital images and related data and includes the tools to use those images. While ARTstor's strengths are most apparent in the fields of art, art history, architecture, visual communication, anthropology and history, ARTstor contains images to support research in many other disciplines. For example, ARTstor contains hundreds of images of structures (buildings, bridges, etc.) relevant in engineering disciplines, as well as hundreds of images in medical fields (anatomy, etc.).

This collection of electronic databases provides access to primary texts in the humanities and social sciences, and cover six broad areas: North American history; Drama, theatre, and film; Women's history and literature; Music; African and African Diaspora history and literature; and Latin American and Latino history and literature. Individual collections include:

* *Women and Social Movements in the United States, 1600-2000*
* *Latino Literature: Poetry, Drama and Fiction*
* *Oral History Online*
* *Twentieth Century North American Drama*
* *North American Women's Drama*
* *North American Theatre Online*
* *Black Drama*
* *American Film Scripts*
* *British and Irish Women's Letters and Diaries*
* *North American Women's Letters and Diaries*
* *North American Immigrant Letters, Diaries and Oral Histories*
* *North American Indian Biographical Database*
* *Black Thought and Culture*
* *Early Encounters in North America: Peoples, Cultures and the Environment*

Classical Music Library

A fully searchable *classical music* resource that includes tens of thousands of licensed recordings that you can listen to over the Internet. Includes music from Medieval to contemporary, from choral works to symphonies, operas and the avant-garde. Audio selections are cross-referenced to a database of supplementary reference information.

THE GLOBE AND MAIL
Canada's Heritage from 1844
brought to you by globeandmail.com

A full-page newspaper archive of *The Globe from 1844* including all the stories, plus thousands of images, advertisements, classifieds, political cartoons, births and deaths from more than 1.4 million pages of Canada's National Newspaper, dating back to the pre-confederation era.

The *Oxford DNB* includes 50,000 biographies of people who shaped the history of the British Isles and beyond, from the earliest times to the year 2002.

Early English Books Online (EEBO) contains page images of virtually every work printed in England, Ireland, Scotland, Wales and British North America and works in English printed elsewhere from 1473-1700–from the first book printed in English by William Caxton, through the age of Spenser and Shakespeare and the tumult of the English Civil War. EEBO contains works by such authors as Malory, Shakespeare, Bacon, Newton, and Galileo and covers a wide range of subject areas including English literature, history, philosophy, linguistics, theology, music, fine arts, education, mathematics, and science.

Eighteenth Century Collections Online (ECCO) is a full-text database that makes available more than 155,000 volumes and over 30 million pages of historical works–in essence, every accessible English-language and foreign-language title published in the United Kingdom between 1701 and 1800, along with thousands of important works from the Americas. Approximately 3,000 of the volumes are French-language titles.

Literature Online (LION) is an extensive library of criticism, reference materials, and primary texts. Literature Online includes 147 full-text literary journals that may be searched or browsed; resources for 16,000 authors; and more than 350,000 primary works–339,000 works of poetry, more than 5,000 plays, and 1,200 key novels and short stories. Literature Online also provides access to the online version of ABELL (Annual Bibliography of English Language and Literature), which indexes journal articles, books, book reviews, and critical editions of scholarship from around the world. ABELL coverage is from the 1920s to present. LION also links into EEBO (Early English Books Online), which provides digital page images for nearly every work printed in England, Ireland, Scotland, Wales, and British North America and works printed in English elsewhere from 1473-1700.

NAXOS offers streaming audio of over 90,000 tracks of music from the Naxos, Marco Polo and Da Capo labels. Genres include classical music, jazz contemporary, jazz/folk/blues legends, nostalgia, world/folk, new age and Chinese music. Nearly 7,000 composers are represented.

Please note: Limit of 5 simultaneous users–please be sure to LOGOUT when finished.

WRDS is an Internet-based business data research service that provides access to Compustat, CRSP, Eventus, Block Regulatory Database, Blockholders, Fama-French Portfolio and Factors, FDIC, Foreign Exchange Rates, Federal Reserve Bank Reports, Penn World Tables, Philadelphia Stock Exchange's United Currency Options Market, and SEC Disclosure Execution databases.

Get IT and Go: Marketing SFX at an Academic Health Science Library

Diana Delgado
Michael A. Wood

INTRODUCTION

Marketing electronic resources to reach the widest population of library users is not easy. While many libraries use a standard range of techniques– Web or e-mail announcements, newsletter articles, and flyers –to advertise their new acquisitions, libraries need to market early and effectively to maximize the efficient use of expensive electronic resources. Although marketing is important and challenging for libraries of all types, librarians receive little formal training in marketing. Books have been written to assist librarians in meeting this challenge, such as *The Visible Librarian: Asserting Your Value with Marketing and Advocacy.*[1] Marketing library purchases is often not viewed as an essential part of the workflow of library staff and faculty, but rather as an "addon" to the work of information professionals.[2] Electronic-resource purchasing budgets usually do not tend to include a corresponding budget item for promotion and evaluation of the resource's usage. When minimal time, money, staff, and resources are invested into promoting a newly acquired resource, it is not surprising that the impact of the marketing is unclear.

In health sciences librarianship, there are efforts to increase the marketing savvy of librarians. The Medical Library Association (MLA) sponsors the public relations Swap and Shop at its annual meeting, which gives attendees the opportunity to share library marketing ideas and samples with colleagues and to discuss marketing tactics with representatives from MLA's public relations firm, Public Communications, Inc.[3] There is also a Library Marketing special interest group that members can join at no charge. Some academic health sciences libraries have added positions focused on marketing, such as Associate Director of Library Marketing and Publications at the Duke University Medical Center Library and Coordinator of Library Marketing at the University of Louisville Kornhauser Health Sciences Library.

The purpose of this case study is to share the experience, sample materials, and lessons learned from involving a wide range of library staff in the implementation and marketing of a new electronic resource,

115

Ex Libris™ SFX® OpenURL technology, at the Weill Cornell Medical Library (WCML).

THE SETTING

Weill Cornell Medical College

The Weill Cornell Medical College (WCMC, formerly Cornell University Medical College), located on the upper east side of Manhattan, was founded in 1898, and has been affiliated with the New York-Presbyterian Hospital (NYPH, formerly The New York Hospital) since 1927. Weill Cornell also has PhD programs in biomedical research and education at the Weill Graduate School of Medical Sciences, and with neighboring Rockefeller University (RU) and the Sloan-Kettering Institute. WCMC maintains affiliations with Memorial Sloan-Kettering Cancer Center (MSKCC), and the Hospital for Special Surgery (HSS), as well as with the metropolitan-area institutions that constitute the New York-Presbyterian Healthcare Network.4,5 In 2001, Cornell University, the parent institution for WCMC, located in Ithaca, New York, established the Weill Cornell Medical College in Qatar (WCMC-Q), a branch of the Weill Cornell Medical College in the country of Qatar.

Weill Cornell Medical Library

The Weill Cornell Medical Library (WCML), consisting of the Samuel J. Wood Library and the C. V. Starr Biomedical Information Center, is the primary information resource in support of teaching, research, and patient care activities of the Medical College, the Graduate School and NYPH. The library emphasizes current, state-of-the-art information with a collection of over 1,500 print periodical subscriptions, approximately 120,000 bound serials volumes, and over 65,000 print monographs. Electronic information resources include over 4,500 electronic journals, over 2,500 books, and more than 100 databases and reference works. The WCML's online catalog, referred to as Tri-Cat (see http://tri-cat.rockefeller.edu/), provides bibliographic access to materials in all formats. Tri-Cat is a shared catalog among the libraries of WMC, RU, MSKCC, and HSS, also known as the 4-Corners consortium. Over 300,000 physical visits each year are made by the more than 12,000 registered faculty, student, and staff from these four institutions. The WCML Web site (see http://library.med.cornell.edu) is an electronic gateway, providing access to Tri-Cat and a searchable and browseable list of electronic journals and networked databases such OVID MEDLINE, PubMed, Web of Science, MicroMedex, UptoDate, and PsycINFO. Online forms allow users to submit recommendations for materials, ask a reference question, submit an interlibrary loan or photocopy request, or leave comments. The library Web site received 11,739,543 hits in 2005. There are 55 networked computer workstations and circulating laptops available in the library for access to the electronic resources. Registered users may also connect to electronic resources remotely through the college's Web-based Virtual Private Network (VPN). Users at the WCMC-Q branch have access to many WCML electronic resources due to the fact that the licenses have been extended to the Distributed e-Library (DeLib), the digital library of WCMC-Q.

History of Promotional Activities

WCML has a history of interest in library promotion activities. From 1991 to 1994, the library had a position called Head of Library Relations that specialized in marketing and public relations regarding library activities with the goals of increasing the library's visibility, strengthening its image, enhancing communications with library users, and improving community relations. During that time, the library created its first promotional characters, including "Sam Starr," who was featured in a computer-based library tour.[6] With the advent of the Web as a way to promote resources and share information, this position was folded into the Information Services program area. Instruction, reference, and information management functions are the responsibility of the Information Services program area, known as the I-Team. The I-Team teaches in the medical school and graduate school curriculum, gives orientations and tours, and provides mediated database searching, and clinical outreach. The curriculum of information classes is promoted on the Web, via e-mail, and on paper schedules and is offered at no charge to all affiliated staff, faculty, and students of the New York-Presbyterian/ Weill Cornell Medical Center. New resources are always highlighted in orientations and classes.

Promotion is always part of the rollout of a newly acquired online resource or library service. It begins with the following efforts typically performed by Information Services staff when they are notified by Collection Development of a new resource. A member of the Information Services staff writes an announcement that describes the resource's scope and uses, comparing it with existing library resources if applicable, and explains how to access it from the library's Electronic Resources page. This announcement is posted on the library's home page. The announcement is also sent out via e-mail through LibNotes, a bi-weekly e-mail distribution list for subscribed users about library news, events, products, and services. LibNotes had 187 subscribers as of June 30, 2006, and the library is currently working to expand the subscriber base. Occasionally promotional handouts and posters created by library staff or provided by the resource vendor will be dispersed throughout the library. The library has a display kiosk in the high-traffic front lounge of the library near the public computer cluster and several bulletin boards that are in less trafficked areas by the photocopiers, in the Microcomputer training room and by the emergency exits.

Successful marketing involves a great deal more than a handful of random promotional activities conducted by a single person or program areas. In order for marketing to meet its objectives of increasing usage and user effectiveness, there must be a high level of commitment by the organization demonstrated by funding and staff participation. This means staff at all levels must work together to fulfill users' immediate and long term expectations.[7] WCML did just that, involving Circulation, Information Services, Collection Development and Computer Services in an all-out marketing extravaganza, a month-long promotional campaign to promote Ex Libris SFX.

GET IT AND SFX DEFINED

Ex Libris SFX OpenURL technology is a unique type of electronic resource for the library to promote. It is not a single topic resource that can be easily explained, and for users it does not exist outside the context of other library resources. The library had previously implemented LinkOut through PubMed and linking to full-text through its other databases, but each implementation worked differently. A single tool was needed to make it easy for users to link to the library's full-text materials regardless of the database being searched. The purpose of the SFX link resolver, from Ex Libris (GET IT, as it is now referred to by all WCML staff and users) is to allow seamless and efficient access to resources and services that are otherwise independent. In other words, SFX brings them together for a one-stop-shopping experience. Library users may not understand what is happening in the background when searching a database, but the appearance of a full-text article or the opportunity to request a copy without having to leave the database saves users time and prevents citation errors in interlibrary loan request forms.

The customized GET IT button, when displayed as shown in Figure 1, provides direct linking to full-text where available, and to other library resources and services from citations within a number of abstracting and in-

FIGURE 1. GET IT button.

Used with permission.

dexing (A&I) databases to which WCML subscribes. SFX technology refers to these databases as "sources." The GET IT button within the sources then links out to the library's other subscribed resources and services, referred to as "targets." Access to the GET IT button is IP or URL driven so that users only see these links if connected to the network, or in the case of PubMed if linking through the library-specific URL.

Some of the WCML's sources, in which GET IT appears, include PubMed, Faculty of 1000, Web of Science, and select databases in OVID. A sample screen shot of GET IT in PubMed is shown in Figure 2. Some of the library's targets include full-text journal packages from Elsevier ScienceDirect, Blackwell Synergy, and SpringerLink; the library's shared online catalog, Tri-Cat; bibliographic reference management tools such as RefWorks and EndNote; and services such as Interlibrary Loan and Document Delivery.

Clicking the GET IT button when displayed in a source as in the PubMed example will open a new browser window with a menu of available targets. Figure 3 shows a sample GET IT menu screen.

In general, the GET IT menu, as implemented by WCML, provides the user with one or more of the following options depending on the availability of full-text:

- *Full-Text:* Links directly to the full-text of the article if the library has a subscription; shows multiple full-text options if the library subscribes through multiple vendors.
- *Holding Information:* Checks Tri-Cat, the shared online catalog, for the availability of the printed material in the Weill Cornell Medical Library or for electronic or print format availability at one of the other 4-Corners libraries.
- *Document Delivery:* Creates a document delivery request for materials in the collection or an interlibrary loan request via WCMC Library's TripSaver service, if neither the full-text nor the printed version is available.

- *Author Search:* Performs an ISI Web of Science author search.
- *Reference Management Tools:* Exports your citation to your RefWorks, EndNote, or Reference Manager software.
- *Help Services:* Provides access to the GET IT frequently asked questions (FAQ) list and the opportunity to e-mail questions or comments to the Information Services staff.

Readings about the SFX link server and OpenURL are available from Ex Libris' Web site at http://www.exlibrisgroup.com/sfx.htm and http://www.exlibris.fr/sfx_openurl.htm.

SFX/GET IT PLANNING AND IMPLEMENTATION

During 2003, the libraries of WCMC, Rockefeller University, Memorial Sloan-Kettering Cancer Center, and the Hospital for Special Surgery, in collaboration with Cold Spring Harbor (CSH) acquired SFX. Although training and purchase were shared amongst the libraries, each library was responsible for setting up its own partition of the server, referred to as an "instance." WMCL shares its instance with the Hospital for Special Surgery, and the GET IT menu is also available to users at the WCMC-Q branch in Qatar.

After the acquisition of SFX, the WCML Web Committee formed a sub-committee that would be responsible for implementation of SFX. The SFX Implementation Committee (SFXIC), which included the heads of Computer Services and Collection Development and the Webmaster, was responsible for the selection of sources, activation of targets, and development of the SFX menu of services. Two full days of training offered by EX Libris in February 2004 were targeted at library staff who would be responsible for the implementation and maintenance of the SFX server and knowledgebase. The Qatar Liaison Librarian and Assistant Head of Collection Development, who joined the library faculty in May 2004 and manages all of the library's electronic resources, later joined the implementation committee.

SFXIC members compiled a list of subscribed databases such as Web of Science, PubMed, OVID (various databases), Faculty of 1000, and the library's catalog, Tri-Cat to review and select as sources for the GET IT button. In addition, a list of full-text resources was reviewed for their availability as targets in the SFX knowledgebase. The criteria for inclusion of the GET IT button in a source were that it had to be OpenURL compliant and the vendor would allow the display of our GET IT button

FIGURE 2. Sample screen of GET IT in PubMed.

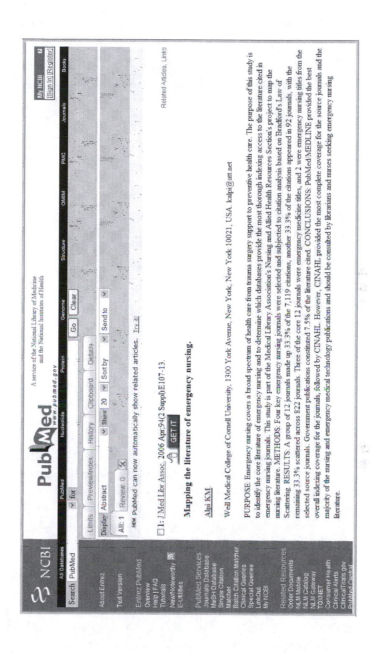

FIGURE 3. Sample GET IT menu screen of resources and services.

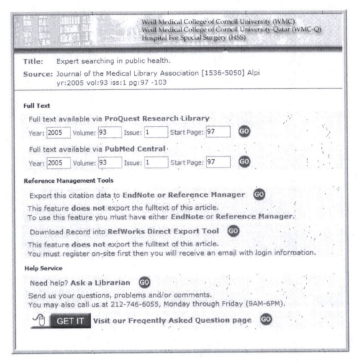

Used with permission.

within the database. Before the GET IT button was added to a source it was therefore determined if the database was OpenURL compliant. All electronic resources containing full-text journals were selected as targets.

After sources were identified and targets were activated, a button to access the services offered by SFX had to be created. Rather than use the generic SFX-supplied button, WCML staff felt creating a button with WCMC colors, similar to the previously developed PubMed LinkOut button, would help users easily distinguish between a library service and a publisher's button or link. An informal survey asked users and staff to consider four different versions of the button placed in a screen shot in the OVID interface and projected for viewing. The buttons read FIND IT or GET IT. Each of the texts appeared with an image of a computer mouse or WCMC windows. The WCMC windows were used often in previous marketing campaigns as the library logo, but that logo was no longer being used on library promotions. GET IT was chosen unanimously by both users and staff.

Once the service was up and running, library staff needed to become familiar with GET IT to promote the service. In-house training was offered by the implementation committee members to all library faculty and staff, emphasizing not only how to utilize the GET IT button but also to be aware of the intricacies and issues of SFX as well as the problem reporting procedure. To help users and staff, the SFXIC created a separate FAQ (Frequently Asked Questions) page for GET IT (see http:// library.med.cornell.edu/Library/HTML/sfxfaq.html) that answers questions such as:

- What is GET IT?
- How do I use GET IT?
- What should I do if there is no full-text available from this service?
- Why does GET IT sometimes show more than one option? Which one should I pick?

MARKETING STRATEGIES

After implementation, lengthy testing, and library staff training, it was evident to Information Services and Circulation staff that users were not aware of the GET IT button in library-subscribed databases or how to use it. The Web Committee and Administration felt that SFX is a technological advancement that would greatly save the user's valuable time in accessing information for education, research and patient care. Now that the service was no longer in beta testing, an SFX Publicity Committee (SFXPC) was appointed by the library director to bring in staff with expertise and interest in promotion. The SFXPC interpreted the charge as a challenge to initiate an aggressive marketing campaign in the promotion and use of SFX via the library's customized GET IT icon. The SFXPC met for three one-hour sessions before proposing "GET IT and GO Day' as the theme for a full day of publicity. The SFXPC decided to base its marketing strategy on the GET IT button. The budget for the promotional campaign was $2000.

SFXPC believed that in order to promote the use of the GET IT button, a number of strategies should be utilized before, during, and after GET IT and GO day. Teasers and buildups were incorporated into the marketing strategy to get people talking about GET IT and to maximize the impact of the GET IT and GO day. The approaches used may seem common sense, but when used in combination and timed strategically, these promotional tactics can reach and retain the attention of a variety of audiences. The following strategies were used:

- *Word-of-Mouth:* Information Services staff were encouraged, a month in advance, to inform users about GET IT, its use, and the upcoming celebration when teaching workshops and while work-ing at the Information Service desk. In addition, the library direc-tor included information about the service and the launch in presentations to WCMC department chairs and the General Fac-ulty Council.
  Staff utilized: All program areas
  Time invested: Ongoing during the course of regular duties
  Added expense: None
- *Announcement via Screen Savers on Public Workstations:* All public workstation computers and laptops, 55 in total, were set up to go idle with display information on GET IT and GO Day de-signed by an SFXPC member a month advance.
  Staff utilized: Computer Services and SFXPC member
  Time invested: 15 hours (security software had to be disabled to add the screensaver and then re-enabled for patron use)
  Added expense: None
- *GET IT Pins* (see Figure 4): One of the first marketing strategies initi-ated by the SFXPC was creation of GET IT and GO pins, that read, "Ask Me How to GET IT @ Your Library." The text of the pins was based on the American Library Association's "@ your library" cam-paign for America's libraries. Many marketing resources can be found on the ALA campaign Web site (see http://www.ala.org/ala/pio/ campaign/campaignamericas.htm) and customized to meet individual library needs. Pins were ordered for all library staff (approximately 35) who were encouraged to wear the pins daily two weeks prior to GET IT and GO Day. The aim was to stimulate users to ask, "What does your pin mean?" This would provide staff members with the opportunity to explain that the library would be celebrating the launch of GET IT, a li-brary service that saves users steps when retrieving full-text materials.
  Staff utilized: Member of SFXPC and Administrative staff
  Time invested: 2 weeks (2 hours for creation and 2 weeks in production)
  Added expense: $63.00
- *E-mail and Listserv Announcements* (see Figure 5): Announce-ments about GET IT and GO Day were made a week in advance on LibNotes and Broadcast e-mail to all WCMC e-mail users.
  Staff utilized: Member of SFXPC
  Time invested: 1 hour
  Added expense: None

- *Web Announcement* (see Figure 6): A week prior to the launch date, an announcement was placed on the library's home page. The day after the event another posting to the library's home page was made announcing the success of the event and offering an online PowerPoint tutorial that had been displayed during GET IT and GO Day (see http://library.med.cornell.edu/Library/ppt/sfxnosound.ppt). Text for announcements was provided by members of the SFXPC.
  Staff utilized: Webmaster
  Added expense: None
  Time invested: 2 hours
- *Information Posters* (see Figure 7): Marketing posters were placed at the Kiosk located at the entrance of the library and also strategically throughout the library (for example, in the commons area where computers and lounge are located) a week prior to launch. Marketing posters detailed the event. One page Information Posters with detailed information on how GET IT works replaced marketing posters on launch date. All posters were created in-house utilizing a color printer.
  Staff utilized: Members of SFXPC
  Time invested: 5 hours
  Added expense: None (printing was done in-house)
- *GET IT Mascot* (see Figure 8): According to Judith A. Siess, author of *The Visible Librarian*, "Two of the most powerful ways to get your message both noticed and remembered are a slogan and a mascot."[8] A human-sized mascot made of polyvinyl chloride (PVC) pipes and plaster of Paris was constructed by a very creative staff member with some attire donated by other library staff. Eli Brary (pronounced "e-library"), our friendly mascot, was placed in the front of the library by a large kiosk highlighting the event. Eli Brary is now used as a visual aid for some of the library's other marketing campaigns.
  Staff utilized: Member of SFXPC
  Time invested: 20 hours over several days
  Added expense: $50
- *Public Address (PA) Announcements:* On GET IT and GO Day, staff members announced the tutorials five minutes before the hour and announced the reception. Circulation and Information Services staff read from a script prepared by SFXPC.
  Staff utilized: Circulation and Information Services
  Time invested: 10 minutes
  Added expense: None
- *Giveaways* (see Figure 9): Five hundred paper clip holders that mimicked the look of a prescription pill bottle were ordered a week in advance to give away at the Circulation Desk and the Facilita-

tion Station on GET IT and GO Day. The holders were embla-
zoned with the library name, URL, phone numbers for the
Information and Circulation desks, and the GET IT button.
Staff utilized: Member of SFXPC and Administrative staff
Time invested: 1 hour for creation and ordering
Added expense: $930

- *Takeaways:* Bookmarks were also offered as takeaways. Along
  with the GET IT image, the bookmark listed the databases from
  which GET IT could be accessed and options available from the
  GET IT menu of services and displayed a picture of a library user,
  with four arms, multitasking (see Figure 7). The drawing was created by a Collection Development staff member who is also a car-
  toonist. It shows that with GET IT one can do so much more. The
  finished 500 bookmarks were available in two weeks. They
  debuted during GET IT and GO Day and are still distributed at the
  Information Desk.

Staff utilized: Members of SFXPC, Collection Development and
Administrative staff
Time invested: 2 hours for creation and ordering
Added expense: $530

FIGURE 4. GET IT pins.

Used with permission.

FIGURE 5. LibNotes posting announcing GET IT and GO Day.

> **LibNotes: Latest News from the Weill Cornell Medical Library, November 10, 2005**
>
> 1) **GET IT** and **GO** Day is Coming
> 2) Art Show Winners
> 3) Podcasts from AccessMedicine
>
> **
> 1) **GET IT** and **GO** Day is Coming
>
> Please join us on Thursday, November 17, as we celebrate the official release of GET IT, a Library service designed to speed your information gathering tasks.
>
> Going from database abstract to full text article? From journal reference to a search of the catalog? From citation to interlibrary loan request? Let GET IT be your timesaving guide.
>
> Come to the Library to learn how GET IT can accelerate your research by eliminating unnecessary steps. Take a brief tutorial and you may win a USB flash drive; watch a slide show and enjoy a slice of GET IT cake; stop by the GET IT and GO station and walk away with a print-out.
>
> Need to know more right now? Check our GET IT Frequently Asked Questions (http://library.med.cornell.edu/Library/HTML/sfxfaq.html), but we also look forward to seeing you in person on GET IT and GO Day.

Used with permission.

"GET IT AND GO" DAY ACTIVITIES

SFXPC felt GET IT and GO Day would be an exciting means for the library to promote GET IT and orient library users to the button and its services. GET IT and GO Day was a celebration of GET IT coming out of beta testing and a formal introduction to library users. In addition to the marketing strategies employed, the library offered a number of activities to users to help familiarize them with the GET IT service. Each activity was developed to illustrate the ease and convenience of utilizing the GET IT button. Activities included:

- *Tutorials:* Instruction was one of the primary goals established by the SFXPC. The committee decided to offer tutorials 15 minutes in length occurring on the hour every hour from 9 a.m. to 5 p.m. in the library conference room. Participants of the tutorials would have an opportunity, by entering a drawing, to win a flashdrive. Prizes were available for every class and winners were announced at the end of each class, assuring audience members stayed for the entire session. In all, eight prizes were awarded to increase incentive to participate.

Staff utilized: Members of SFXPC, Information Services and Collection Development

Time invested: 4 hours total (2 hours during the event and 2 hour preparation)

Added expense: $200 (8 flashdrive prizes)

- *Slide Show* (see Figure 10): A desktop computer with a 19″ flat-screen monitor was placed in the Lounge area between the Facilitation Station and the tables holding the cakes. A three-minute long PowerPoint slide show with music ran in a loop on the computer. Users who joined the reception or passed by were attracted to the sound and able to view the slide show for a quick overview of the new service. A version of the slide show, without audio, is posted on the Library's Web site at http://library.med.cornell.edu/ Library/ppt/sfxnosound.ppt.

  Staff utilized: Members of SFXPC and Computer Services

  Time invested: 3 hours

  Added expense: None

- *Facilitation Station* (see Figure 11): Users waiting for computers were assisted by a staff person, who was serving as a facilitator. Articles were printed on the users' behalf. Users received brief (4-5minutes) orientations to GET IT during the transactions at one of the two facilitation desks and were encouraged to attend the tutorials. The paper clip holders and the bookmarks were distributed.

  Staff utilized: Members of SFXPC, Information Services and Collection Development

  Time invested: 8 hours (During the entire day's event)

  Added expense: None

- *Reception* (see Figure 12): A reception was held between noon and 3 p.m., the library's busiest hours, in the lounge area of the library where eating is permitted. Sheet cakes emblazoned with the GET IT logo (see Figure 13), chips, pretzels, and beverages were served to attendees. The library director and several other staff distributed over 150 pieces of cake.

  Staff utilized: Members of SFXPC, Collection Development, Circulation and Administration

  Time invested: 4 Hours (3 hour reception and 1 hour set-up/clean-up)

  Added expense: $500 (Costs include food, beverages, utensils, and decorations)

FIGURE 6. Home page announcing GET IT and GO Day.

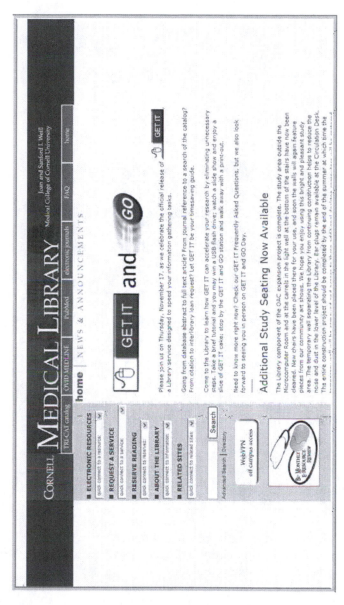

Used with permission.

FIGURE 7. Marketing posters.

Used with permission.

LESSONS LEARNED AND FUTURE DIRECTIONS

The acquisition of Ex Libris SFX provided an opportunity to develop and implement a creative promotional campaign. This promotion has had a lasting effect on the staff who participated. These are exciting times for WCML. Advancements in technology provide the opportunity to promote and expand educational roles, programs, and services. It is important that these be marketed in novel and interesting ways to attract as many users as possible. One of the lessons learned is that creativity has costs and that the budgeting needs to be overestimated; the final expenditures for the promotion exceeded the budget. The success of GET IT and GO Day has led staff to re-think and improve marketing tactics

FIGURE 8. Kiosk and mascot Eli Brary.

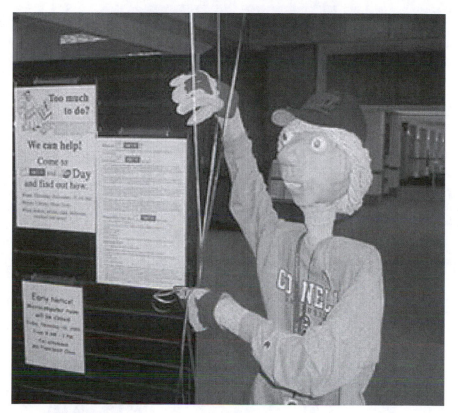

Used with permission.

for future promotions of electronic resources. Since the launch of GET IT the feedback from users has been anecdotal, but positive. In January 2006, an article written by an SFXPC member was published in *InsideCUL,* [9] an online newsletter, to reach colleagues on the Cornell University main campus in Ithaca, New York who are currently implementing OpenURL technology.

The WCML staff plan to provide further instruction on GET IT and other electronic resources, via the library's Web site, by creating interactive video tutorials using various applications, such as Camtasia. WCML staff will also continue to educate users through workshops and orientation programs and by word of mouth. In the future, Weill Cornell Medical Library will incorporate user surveys and focus groups as

FIGURE 9. Sample giveaway.

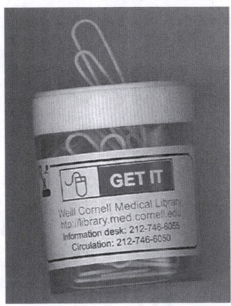

Used with permission.

FIGURE 10. Attendees viewing slide show.

Used with permission.

FIGURE 11. Information Services staff at the Facilitation Stations.

Used with permission.

FIGURE 12. The GET IT and GO Day reception in the Library's front lounge.

Used with permission.

FIGURE 13. One of the GET IT and GO Day cakes.

Used with permission.

Wakimoto, Walker, and Dabbour described in their article, "The Myths and Realities of SFX in Academic Libraries,"[10] to better evaluate the impact marketing has on users, and to obtain comments on how successful users are in working with the technology.

NOTES

1. Siess, Judith A, *The Visible Librarian: Asserting Your Value with Marketing and Advocacy* (Chicago: American Library Association, 2003).

2. Brewerton, Antony, "Inspired! Award-winning Library Marketing," *New Library World* 104, no. 7/8 (2003): 267-277.

3. An Abundance of Promotional Ideas Shine at 2006 MLA Swap and Shop. <http://www.mlanet.org/press/2006/june06.html#2> (accessed June 30, 2006)

4. Weill Medical College <http://www.med.cornell.edu/about/> (accessed April 14, 2006).

5. Cornell University Weill Medical College <http://www.cornell.edu/visiting/nyc/weill.cfm> (accessed April 14, 2006).

6. Sienkiewicz, Daniel M., M. Buckwalter, and Helen-Ann Brown. "A Sam Starr Mystery: Building a Computerized Tour for the Library." In: *User Education in Health Sciences Libraries: A Reader,* edited by Sandra Wood. (New York: Haworth Press, 1995), 281-289.

7. Dillon, Dennis, "Strategic Marketing of Electronic Resources," *Acquisitions Librarian* 14 no. 28 (2002): 117-134.

8. Siess, Judith. A. *The Visible Librarian, 62.*

9. Merlo, Loretta. "GET IT (SFX) Launched at Weill Cornell Medical Library," *InsideCUL* (January 2006) Available: http://www.library.cornell.edu/insidecul/200601/shorts.html

10. Wakimoto, Jina Choi., David S. Walker, and Katherine S. Dabbour, "The Myths and Realities of SFX in Academic Libraries," *The Journal of Academic Librarianship* 32 no. 2 (2006): 127-136.

Hitting the Spot: Marketing Federated Searching Tools to Students and Faculty

Christopher Cox

Federated searching, also known as simultaneous or cross-database searching, has been widely publicized as the librarian's answer to Google. As is demonstrated by the most recent OCLC survey, 89% of college student information searches begin with a search engine, and the search engine of choice is Google (62%).[1] For years, library pundits like Lippincott have been urging libraries to respond to the Google threat and the needs of the Millennial generation. They want the search process to be simple and the results to come fast, something that is not the case in today's libraries "where students must make separate searches of the online catalog and every database of potential interest, after first identifying which databases might be relevant."[2] As Luther trumpets in her article, "Trumping Google," federated searching meets "the Google generation's" expectations in terms of the time and quality of results they are willing to accept.[3] Users type keywords in a Googlelike search box, yielding results from various full-text library collections. Many libraries have jumped on the federated search bandwagon, recognizing its potential to drive more users to library Web sites and its ability to dramatically increase usage of expensive electronic library resources.

The University of Wisconsin-Eau Claire was no exception, and in spring 2005, our implementation of MetaLib, SearchSpot, was rolled out the public. Despite the marketing potential of federated search to notify students of the library's electronic content, how could we, with a small budget and limited staff, compete with an established, popular product such as Google? How could we effectively get the word out about SearchSpot–letting students know the time savings and benefits of going to one place to search for resources which are more scholarly than those located through Google and which were paid for with their tuition dollars? This article will explain step-by-step what we did. While we may not have truly trumped Google as the first choice for information, our campaign was successful in driving traffic to the product and in reaching out to our students.

LITERATURE REVIEW

The literature regarding federated searching is in its infancy, so it comes as no surprise that there aren't many published accounts of successful marketing campaigns for federated search engines. When it comes to marketing, there has been only the occasional mention in implementation accounts of the need for publicity, or brief descriptions of marketing strategies such as Boston College's "Top Ten Reasons to Use MetaQuest."[4]

There has been discussion of federated search engine marketing in the gray literature, however. Hamblin and Stubbings[5] mention a variety of advertising techniques used to market their MetaLib implementation, including "messages to staff and student e-mail bulletin boards, a press release in their library news sheet, posters and printed flyers, pens, an article in the University news publication, a display in the foyer of the library, a newsflash on the University's home page and an official launch event including a brief demonstration." In a presentation delivered at the 2005 Chalmers University Annual Library Seminar, Tuomaala details training and marketing efforts aimed at specific stakeholders/user groups.[6] For example, students at Helsinki University of Technology learned about MetaLib primarily via instruction in First Year Experience classes and other courses. Faculty gained information from sessions conducted in departments and through mailing list posts.

Another trend in federated search marketing is the catchy name. The University of Pittsburgh christened their WebFeat implementation Zoom![7] Librarians chose the name because it illustrated the product's speed and ease of use. The library worked with the university's marketing department to come up with branding and a slogan: "Zoom! . . . any easier and it wouldn't be doing research." Once Zoom! had been seamlessly integrated into the library's Web pages, the marketing campaign began full force, including "an array of promo materials like postcards, clingform stickers, tabletop signs and mousepads."

BRANDING

The implementation of MetaLib at the University of Wisconsin-Eau Claire began with the appointment of a task force, charged with configuring the search interface to the software, adding our resources, and organizing them into categories. Following the University of Pittsburgh's lead, in fall 2004 the MetaLib implementation task force asked the library's marketing and promotions committee to come up with a name and brand for the service. The committee brainstormed names which ranged from the expected (metasearch, simulsearch) to the bizarre (McEntireSearch, findasaurus). After consultation with library staff and students assistants, the committee recommended SearchSpot as the service's new name. The name was not the staff's favorite, but was chosen because it best described the service, was similar to search engine names like Google, and immediately evoked numerous ideas for promotional materials and campaigns. In her article about Google's marketing strategies and what the library can learn from them, Lee supports our decision, stating that brand names should be "easy to spell and recall, convey major benefits, be distinctive in nature, and be compatible for all service or product offerings."[8] SearchSpot certainly meets all these criteria. The Web Librarian then created the SearchSpot logo (see Figure 1), which was later incorporated into the design of the search interface and would be used to market the product on the Web site and on all promotional materials.

PROMOTION: PHASE I

SearchSpot was released to the public in spring 2005. However, as many libraries have chosen to do, we began with a soft rollout, hoping to work out all the bugs in the system and appease some of the more skeptical library staff members in the process. The marketing and promotions committee followed the library's lead with an equivalent "soft" or preliminary promotional campaign. The author first contacted the heads of the university's 32 academic departments and met with ten of them in spring 2005. SearchSpot was demonstrated to each, and they were asked to share it with their faculty and to try it out themselves, offering any feedback they might have. In March 2005, an announcement was added to our library's home page, coordinated with the publication of an article in both our semiannual print newsletter, *Off the Shelf*, and our monthly e-newsletter, *The McIntyre Advantage*, both aimed at faculty.

Faculty members were targeted first primarily because we felt they would be best at notifying their students. However, as we later learned by speaking with faculty about SearchSpot, most had not seen the publications and did not know of SearchSpot's existence. Students were almost completely ignored in this initial campaign, save a few librarians who were already introducing SearchSpot in their information literacy sessions.

FIGURE 1. SearchSpot Logo

Used with permission.

In October 2005, we added a link to SearchSpot to our databases pages. We also added SearchSpot as a search option on our home page Quick Search box. In November 2005 we once again included an article in *Off the Shelf*, this time attempting to fine tune our message to communicate those aspects of SearchSpot faculty would find most appealing. Still, search statistics of SearchSpot showed a mediocre rise, at best.

PROMOTION: PHASE II

The lack of success with this method of "hit and miss" marketing led us to sharpen our focus and reorganize our promotional efforts. We decided that we needed a plan for the more vigorous spring 2006 promotional campaign. The plan would list the overall promotional methods, address all our target audiences, and provide messages, specific communication vehicles, a schedule or sequence of promotional activities, and an overall cost of the campaign, as well as some method of assessment of its success.[9] The plan and budget we composed are included as Appendix A and B.

PROMOTION PLAN

Target Audience

The marketing and promotions committee first identified SearchSpot's target audience. The federated searching literature shows that there is some disagreement on this, with librarians in surveys conducted by McCaskie[10] and RLG[11] suggesting that undergraduates, particularly first-year students, are the target audience, while Cervone[12] and others have noted the value of federated search products for graduate students and faculty. Thus, we decided to conduct two distinct campaigns: one targeting students and one targeting faculty. The campaigns would be multi-pronged, utilizing a variety of communication vehicles to inform the target audiences about SearchSpot.

Message

In our promotional materials, the message would be different for each of the target markets. The committee had previously undertaken a stakeholder analysis and listed the needs of the various groups and the services that would fulfill them. When it came to the messages we would deliver to students, we focused on what we knew about the characteristics of the Millennial generation and their approach to research. As Manuel noted in her review of the literature on first-year students, Millennials look for research solutions which save them time, offer fewer choices, "good enough" search results and do just enough to get a passing grade.[13] They are pressed for time and look for "the easiest, least painful way to complete a research project in a timely and satisfactory fashion."[14] As mentioned above, many of students' needs are addressed by federated searching. Tallent,[15] in his usability study, noted that students' habits with federated searching showed no significant change from what had been previously observed. With this data in hand, we chose to emphasize three things to our students: that SearchSpot allows them to search multiple, discipline-specific full-text library resources from one place; that searching it was Google-like, quick and easy, and thus the research process would be easier, less time-consuming, and less painful than before; and full-text access to the item was only one click away utilizing our SFX implementation, FindIt.

For faculty, we offered a different message. Knowing they were equally overscheduled, we did emphasize the time savings in searching selected resources using one interface, but we concentrated more on the ease of performing multi-disciplinary research, on personalization features like personal resource lists and search alerts, and on integrating the library's resources more fully within our course management system, Desire2Learn.

Communication Vehicles

The marketing and promotions committee had previously listed the various communication vehicles available. In print, we would advertise to both students and faculty in a variety of ways. Like Hamblin and Stubbings, we would put up posters in the library and around campus, and place table tents on tables in campus dining areas. We would personally sell SearchSpot by staffing a table in the campus center where we would give out free pens, promotional literature, demonstrate SearchSpot, and answer questions. On the Web, we would better integrate SearchSpot into our databases pages, using SearchSpot to generate our database A-Z and databases by discipline lists, and more prominently linking it from our home page.

For students specifically, we would advertise in the student newspaper, *The Spectator*, and SearchSpot would be personally sold in library tours and in information literacy sessions. Faculty would be targeted through personal selling at presentations to the Network for Teaching Excellence (NET) and in individual department meetings. We would also create promotional handouts for distribution, along with the pens, to faculty at these meetings.

Mascot

Upon further consideration, the committee decided we needed to have a unifying theme for the campaign, one that would appeal to both audiences and could be included on all vehicles. We settled on a mascot as the best way of doing this. The previous year, we had witnessed Career Services' successful campaign for its "Explore Your Possibilities" program, where students learn about various career choices. They introduced a mascot for the event, "Possibility Pete," through a series of ads in *The Spectator*, pathway signs around campus, and stress balls shaped like Pete. The campaign was so successful that students stole the pathway signs. We wanted our SearchSpot campaign to be just as successful.

The author created a rough sketch, a cross between the old Seven-Up one-spot and an M&M. We gave it to the University's graphic artist, who came up with what is pictured in Figure 2. As you will see, we used the logo in all our print advertising. We were unable to afford stress balls in the spot shape and could not use path signs like Career Services as it was winter when we did our campaign and the ground was frozen.

Schedule of Promotional Activities

We decided to start the SearchSpot promotional campaign at the beginning of spring semester 2006. The advertising campaign would last four weeks, with personal selling continuing the remainder of the semester. Different vehicles would be used each week, starting with three

FIGURE 2. SearchSpot Mascot

Spectator ads which would build awareness of the service, followed by posters and a table in the campus center, and finally the table tents in the campus food service areas.

Cost

A preliminary budget was crafted which included the cost for all advertising, including printing costs, cost of the *Spectator* ads, and promotional pens. The total was estimated at about $250, with the pens being the most expensive ($140) and accounting for over 60% of the overall cost of the campaign, followed by printing costs ($65) and the cost of the three *Spectator* ads ($50). See Appendix B for budget worksheet.

Assessment

The marketing and promotions committee would assess the success of the campaign in two ways: an analysis of SearchSpot usage and a student survey conducted near the end of the semester.

CAMPAIGN IMPLEMENTATION

With the plan in place, we got to work on putting it into action. The pens were ordered and we implemented the changes to the library Web site, having the SearchSpot software generate our database A-Z and databases by discipline lists. While this wasn't officially a marketing decision, we knew that driving users to the SearchSpot interface, even if it just consisted of clicking on a link to an individual database, would drive traffic to the site and would let users gain familiarity with it. We expected some complaints as a result of the change, but received relatively few.

Next, the author presented SearchSpot to NET. The presentation consisted of a brief PowerPoint followed by a demonstration of SearchSpot. NET staff were excited by the service and offered ideas of how faculty could integrate it into their existing lessons. NET also maintains Desire2Learn, so contacts were made in this meeting to set up assistance for faculty interested in integrating SearchSpot content into their course sites.

After that, the 32 department heads were again contacted, this time asking for ten minutes in their department's meetings to talk about SearchSpot. Twelve departments (mostly in the humanities and management) expressed interest. A handout was created which shared the faculty messages, including its compatibility with Desire2Learn. The mascot was prominently displayed on the handouts. In the live demonstration of SearchSpot, the author showed the search box on the library home page, then the list of resources for the department's discipline and conducted a search of selected resources within it. The personalization features (how to save the search as a search alert and how to save specific results) were then explained. A Web page created by one of our staff members was also presented which generates URLs and search box code to specific databases and disciplines, linking into Desire2Learn.[16] SearchSpot pens were also distributed.

These presentations were extremely successful. Through them we reached 213 faculty members, 42% of the total faculty at the university. Many of the faculty had already tried SearchSpot and many had interesting questions and suggestions for improvement. Overall, the meetings were a good public relations vehicle as well, since faculty often shared other concerns they had about the library.

We created the three *Spectator* ads (an example of which is shown in Figure 3) following the Career Services example. The idea was to gradually reveal the logo and message over the three ads, building awareness of the service. All three were published, but there were problems with the size of the ads, and communication with the student editors

FIGURE 3. Example *Spectator* Ad Introducing SearchSpot to Students

Introducing SearchSpot

SearchSpot lets you search
multiple library resources at once.

McIntyre Library. Your Information Advantage.

wasn't easy. The ads ran in late January and early February and, unlike the Career Services campaign, resulted in little buzz.

The day the last *Spectator* ad went to press, we added the SearchSpot mascot to the library home page, linking users to the service. The author created the 11x17 posters in Microsoft Publisher with the logo, mascot, and message, "search multiple library resources at one time." The posters were printed and put up on bulletin boards in buildings throughout the campus, and remained up for the semester. Laminated versions of the posters were also put up in the elevators and on the library's circulation desk, visible when one entered the library.

The next day, librarians took shifts staffing a table in the campus center for three hours during the lunch rush. The table had a banner and posters announcing SearchSpot, a handout created with our message to students, and free pens for distribution, and a laptop on the wireless network was used for live demonstrations of SearchSpot. The experience was quite positive. During the three hours, we gave out 100 handouts and over 400 pens. Some students listened to our spiel about SearchSpot and many stayed for a brief demonstration. Surprisingly, many students mentioned that they already knew about SearchSpot and had used it for previous assignments. They seemed overwhelmingly positive in their reaction to the new service.

The final step in the print advertising campaign was the table tents, also created by the author in Publisher. Since the three days we were able to get permission to display the materials were around Valentine's Day, we decided to go with a valentine's theme, and the message: "Not sure where to start your research? You'll love SearchSpot!"

The data surrounding presentations of SearchSpot in information literacy sessions is a bit sketchy. It's not clear how many of the library faculty introduced SearchSpot into their spring sessions. As has been recorded in the literature, our institution embodies the argument described by Bell[17] between the Googleizers and the Resistors. According to Bell, Googleizers want to "satiate the end user's need for an easy, convenient gateway" to our full-text databases. The hope is that if the interface is more user friendly, our resources will get more use, and students will find what they need to complete their research.[18] Resistors, on the other hand, believe that the "dumbed down interfaces" of federated search systems, which offer limited searching options and do not encourage critical thinking concerning resource choice or search preparation, will impede student information literacy.[19]

The disagreement on our campus also involves the choice of MetaLib, a decision made by the University of Wisconsin system and purchased for the libraries. Some library faculty at UW-Eau Claire question whether the software is ready to teach, since it currently recalculates search result numbers each time the screen is refreshed, and has no peer-reviewed limit, along with other flaws. Couple this with the faculty's unfamiliarity with the software and thus their trepidation in presenting it, a complaint McCaskie and Lampert and Dabbour[20] have previously recorded, and you understand why some may not be eager to introduce SearchSpot to their students.

The few who did teach SearchSpot emphasized the service more in lower-level undergraduate classes like English Composition. Knowing Millennials' need for fewer choices and students' unfamiliarity with our resources, they favored demonstrating the librarian-selected groupings of resources by discipline over the selection of individual resources in a particular category.

ASSESSMENT

As was already mentioned, the response to SearchSpot by students and faculty was almost overwhelmingly positive. Their satisfaction with the service is confirmed by their use of it. MetaLib offers the ability to generate statistical reports through the "Reports and Statistics" function of the administrative module. The reports of most interest to the author were those which detailed the number of searches conducted in the software and the number of native interface referrals from SearchSpot. The timeframe selected was the university's nine-month academic year, September 2005 to May 2006. The author hoped that the reports would show a statistically significant increase in the number of searches conducted and referrals.

A chart showing the SearchSpot searches and native interface referrals per month appears as Figure 4. Prior to February 2006, SearchSpot searches were relatively flat, averaging about 14,000 searches a month. The same was the case for native interface referrals from September to December, with the number of referrals averaging 158. A statistically significant jump occurred in SearchSpot searches in February, resulting in a fivefold increase in the number of searches conducted (15,643 searches in January compared to 83,299 in February), just at the time the promotional campaign was in full swing. An increase of roughly 29,000 was recorded in both March and April, prior to a drop when students had completed their papers and then left campus for summer break.

FIGURE 4. Marketing Impact on SearchSpot Searches and Native Interface Referrals

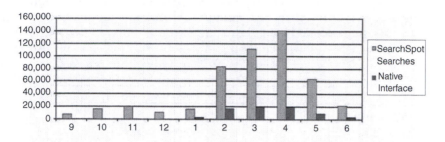

Enormous increases were also noted in native database referrals between December and January (twenty-twofold increase) and January and February (fivefold increase), with about 1000 more referrals recorded in both March and April before the drop off for summer break. Like Loughborough University, which witnessed a 609% increase in database searches,[21] UW-Eau Claire also noted a dramatic increase in database searches.

It's hard to predict whether the campaign actually made a difference in increasing the numbers of searches or referrals. The other big change that could account for the increase was the generation of the database lists by SearchSpot, thus forcing people to use SearchSpot to search the native interface of our databases. However, it's hard to believe that the promotional campaign had no part in this increase.

In an effort to determine not only if our campaign was successful overall, but also what aspects we should continue, we composed a survey. The survey consisted of six questions, asking students how they first heard about SearchSpot and listing the various communication vehicles we had employed in our most recent promotional campaign, three questions concerning the SearchSpot mascot, and one demographic question about their status on campus (students, faculty, staff or other). The survey was created using the freely available SurveyMonkey.com, so it could be distributed electronically.

The original intent was to deliver the survey via e-mail to a random sample of undergraduates. The university has strict human subject rules, and each survey proposal must be reviewed by the Institutional Review Board, a process which takes about a month. Due to time constraints, the author had no choice but to employ a more haphazard approach. Surveys were gathered in three ways: a link was posted on the library Web site and an announcement put in the library's monthly student e-newsletter. This garnered about six responses. An e-mail was next sent to all library student supervisors, asking student workers to fill out the survey. This yielded 45 more surveys. Finally, in order to gain a more representative campus sample, copies of the survey were printed and distributed to willing parties outside various academic buildings throughout campus (six in all) during the second-to-last week of classes. 94 surveys were collected using this method. This brought the total to 145 completed surveys. The majority of survey respondents (n = 135 or 94%) were students, with only 2 faculty members and 6 staff members completing the survey. Student responses were the primary target of the survey, so this result was satisfactory for us.

The survey provided some interesting data. In terms of notifying the target population of the existence of SearchSpot, of those surveyed only 64 of 145 (44%) had never heard of SearchSpot. When it came to communication vehicles, ironically the posters in the library (21%) were the most effective, followed by the library Web site announcement (18%), instruction sessions (13%), and word of mouth (11%). The most expensive vehicles–the pens and the *Spectator* ads–were the least seen–10% and 4% respectively.

The majority of students (61%) were familiar with SearchSpot, showing they had heard about it or, if they guessed the answer, perhaps serving as an endorsement of the name we chose. When it came to the mascot, which some library staff felt was unnecessary, the survey results show a great deal of student recognition and satisfaction. 99 of 145 (68%) had seen the SearchSpot mascot, 79% liked it or had no opinion, and 65% felt we should continue with the mascot.

It is hard to say whether the results of the survey were truly representative. The university enrolls a total of 10,063 students, meaning only 1% of the total student body were polled. The timing of the survey, near the end of the semester, may also have resulted in a low return rate. Other factors may also skew the results. With 35% of the surveys possibly generated within the library, it's not surprising that the vehicles inside the library were seen as more effective than those outside, like the *Spectator* ads. The results also seem in conflict with what OCLC's recent survey of college students found concerning how they learn about electronic information resources.[21] The most popular way of finding out about new electronic information resources was from a friend (67%), with the library Web site (35%) and notification from a librarian (34%) appearing far down the list.

LESSONS LEARNED

All in all, our campaign was marginally successful. Here are a few helpful hints to keep in mind when developing a campaign:

1. *Plan early!* Marketing and promotion take time, no matter what you are promoting. Be sure to plan ahead, especially concerning such things as table tents, tables, or rooms, which may need to be reserved months in advance.

2. *Beware of hidden costs.* Be sure you create a budget and get it approved prior to beginning the campaign. Also, make sure you are clear about the cost of each vehicle. The author was recently surprised by a $145 bill from the university's graphics artist for the creation of the SearchSpot mascot, something the author thought was being prepared at no cost.

3. *Always build in assessment.* Marketing is expensive. Make sure you know just how successful it is–plan to assess the campaign so you can make adjustments in the future.

CONCLUSION

Overall, despite a few bumps along the way, we are very happy with our campaign for SearchSpot. Libraries are continually being asked to justify their existence and to demonstrate the benefits they provide. Federated search software, despite all its advantages, is expensive and a labor intensive enterprise to get up and running. In order for such products to be a success on campus, libraries need to make an effort to get the word out about them, telling their users the benefits and possible drawbacks of using them. Libraries will also need to assess the success, not only of the promotional campaigns which will attract users to the new search engine, but the federated search engines themselves, to understand how users conduct searches and to solve any problems they may encounter. It stands to reason that, if federated searching actually fulfills the needs of Millennials as advertised, then advertisement of the software will help students to adopt it and, hopefully, generate greater interest in the library resources and result in greater satisfaction with the library as a whole.

REFERENCES

1. OCLC. *Perceptions of Libraries and Information Resources* (2006). Available: <http://www.oclc.org/reports/2005perceptions.htm> (June 5, 2006).

2. Lippincott, Joan K. "Net Generation Students & Libraries." *EDUCAUSE Review* (March/April 2005): 56-6.

3. Luther, Judy. "Trumping Google: Metasearching's Promise." *Library Journal* 128, 16 (October 1, 2003): 36-9.

4. Gerrity, Bob, Theresa Lyman and Ed Tallent. "Blurring Services and Resources: Boston College's Implementation of MetaLib and SFX." *Reference Services Review* 30, 3 (2002): 229-241.

5. Hamblin, Yvonne and Ruth Stubbings. *The Implementation of MetaLib and SFX at Loughborough University Library*, October 2003. Available: <http://www.jisc.ac.uk/uploaded_documents/Metalibcasestudy.pdf> (February 15, 2006).

6. Tuomaala, Tiina. "Experiences of SFX and Metalib at Helsinki University of Technology (TKK)," *2005 Chalmers University Annual Library Seminar, September 28, 2005, Goteborg, Finland.* Available: <http://www.lib.chalmers.se/konferenser/chals2005/docs/tuomaala.ppt> (July 5, 2006).

7. WebFeat. "University of Pittsburgh Upgrades Custom Branded WebFeat System." July 20, 2005. Available: <http://www.webfeat.org/releases/1Jul05_Pittsburgh.htm> (July 5, 2006).

8. Lee, Deborah. "Checking out the Competition: Marketing Lessons from Google." *Library Administration & Management* 20, 2 (Spring 2006): 94-5.

9. Association of College and Research Libraries (ACRL) and 3M Systems. *Strategic Marketing for Academic and Research Libraries Participant Manual* (1995). Available: <http://www.ala.org/ala/acrl/acrlissues/marketingyourlib/ParticipantManual.doc> (July 5, 2006).

10. McCaskie, Lucy. *What are the Implications for Information Literacy Training in Higher Education with the Introduction of Federated Search Tools?* Master's Thesis, University of Sheffield, 2004.

11. Research Libraries Group (RLG). *Report on RLG Metasearch Survey*, 2005. Available: <http://www.rlg.org/en/page.php?Page_ID=20750> (July 5, 2006).

12. Cervone, Frank. "What We've Learned from Doing Usability Testing on OpenURL Resolvers and Federated Search Engines." *Computers in Libraries* 25, 9 (October 2005): 10-14.

13. Manuel, Kate. "What Do First-Year Students Know about Information Research? And What Can We Teach Them?" *Proceedings of the ACRL Twelfth National Conference, April 7-10, 2005, Minneapolis, Minnesota:* 401-17.

14. Valentine, Barbara. "The Legitimate Effort in Research Papers: Student Commitment Versus Faculty Expectations." *Journal of Academic Librarianship* 27, 2 (March 2001): 107-15.

15. Tallent, Ed. "Metasearching in Boston College Libraries–A Case Study of User Reactions." *New Library World* 105, 1/2 (2004): 69-75.

16. Hillis, Daniel. "SearchSpot Search Box & Link Generator," February 2, 2006. Available: <http://lib1.uwec.edu/searchspot/SSSearchBoxGenerator.asp> (July 5, 2006).

17. Bell, Steven J. "Submit or Resist: Librarianship in the Age of Google." *American Libraries.* 36, 9 (October 2005): 68-71.

18. Bell, 69.

19. Frost, William. "Do We Want or Need Metasearching?" *Library Journal* 129, 6 (April 1, 2004): 68.

20. Lampert, Lynn and Kathy Dabbour. "Falling Down the Portal: Adventures in Federated Metasearch Technology at California State University Northridge." LITA National Forum, San Jose, California, October 1, 2005. Available: <http://library.csun.edu/llampert/LITA/litaslides.ppt> (June 20, 2006).

21. Hamblin and Stubbings, 15.

22. OCLC.

APPENDIX A
Marketing Plan Worksheet

Title of the Event: SearchSpot Promotion–Phase II

Date of Event: January-March 2006

What message(s) do we wish to communicate?
–SearchSpot is a new product that allows users to search multiple library resources from one place
–SearchSpot is a Google-like, quick and easy way to search the variety of resources the library has to offer
–SearchSpot is a good place to start searching if you're not sure where the best place is to find information

Who is the target audience?
Students, Faculty with separate campaigns for each

What is the time frame?
–Begin planning November and complete over winter break
–Divide up responsibilities among marketing committee members
–Communication using a variety of vehicles to let students know SearchSpot exists and what it has to offer

Why communicate? What do we want people to do as a result?
–Use SearchSpot
–Find the information they are looking for
–Offer us feedback on the value of the product and how we can improve it

What activities/publications/events are associated with the plan?

All:
January 2006-
–Presentation to Teaching and Learning Department faculty
–Database lists (categories, A-Z list) now generated by SearchSpot

Students:
January 2006-
–SearchSpot mascot created and unveiled in series of three ads in *The Spectator*
–Librarians add SearchSpot to lesson plans for every information literacy class they teach

February 2006-
–Table in campus center to distribute student literature, promotional pens
–Posters with mascot go up in academic buildings and dorms, additional posters added in elevators, on circulation desk, and throughout library
–SearchSpot mascot added to library home page
–Table tents with mascot placed in all dining halls

Faculty:
Spring 2006-
Presentation at faculty meetings to introduce SearchSpot
Develop way for faculty to create direct links to SearchSpot categories or search boxes into SearchSpot to be added to course web sites

What resources are required (funds, skills, staff time, temporaries, consultants)?
–Funding for pens, printing, *Spectator* advertising
–Time (planning, creating marketing materials, implementing marketing, conducting survey/assessment)

Who has primary responsibility?
–Marketing Committee

Who are our collaborators, helpers/ supporters?
–Library staff and students
–*The Spectator*
–University Graphics department

How will we evaluate/measure the success of the plan?
–Increased usage of SearchSpot (MetaLib Admin statistics module)
–Surveys to see if students have used it, noted the publicity, liked the logo.

Created 0905 CC

APPENDIX B

Budget Estimate Worksheet–SearchSpot Promotion Phase II				
Time	**Item**	**Amount**	**Cost per item**	**Total**
Supplies/Materials	Posters (11×17)	34	$ 0.04	$ 22.61
	Handout–Faculty	100	will copy ourselves	$ -
	Handout–Students	100	will copy ourselves	$ -
	Table tents	448		$ 17
	Posters for Elevators (laminated)	3	$ 2	$ 11
	Pens	500		$ 140.00
	Spectator Advertising	3	$3.45 per inch / 5 inches	$ 52
Space Rental				
Refreshments				
Other expenses				
TOTAL				$ 242.06

Infiltrating NetGen Cyberculture: Strategies for Engaging and Educating Students on Their Own Terms

Gail M. Golderman
Bruce Connolly

INTRODUCTION

At one time, marketing a product or service meant erecting a billboard by the side of the road and hoping that one's intended audience would drive by and take notice. Now, in order to cut through the overload of information, those signs have to be located everywhere your audience might happen to look. In similar fashion, having an impressive and centrally located building on campus (with a virtual monopoly on academic information) was about all it took to reach the students the library served. Now, the library's presence also has to be both more direct and more pervasive if we expect to engage the Internet generation of students.

This chapter examines several initiatives that the Union College Library is pursuing in its efforts to connect directly with today's NetGen student. Our aim has been, first, to promote the library's services and electronic resources, and ultimately, to educate our students (as well as our faculty) in how to use these resources effectively. Besides the messages–educational and social–that our efforts are attempting to send, the strategies we have adopted for marketing our resources include:

- Utilizing iTunes file sharing to promote music resources as a way of finding a comfortable common ground for engagement while enhancing the library's image as a diverse and valuable resource. (This article also describes Schaffer Library's efforts to add value and attractiveness to Web OPAC records with such elements as links to audio samples, CD reviews, and artist biographies);
- Opening the lines of communication via podcasting, the library blog, and RSS feeds as the logical, and potentially interactive, extension of the library's online newsletter;

- Meeting student researchers on their own terms via efforts to encourage a shift from Google to Google Scholar as a viable research
tool thanks to the deep-linking capabilities of Open WorldCat and
Serials Solutions, while still teaching and promoting the use of the
catalog and more traditional electronic resources. Both approaches
are incorporated into library instruction sessions and include an e-
mailed research guide (with embedded links to the sources presented in the classroom) that we send out as a follow-up to the formal instruction session; and
- Identifying librarians as a resource and making them more visible
and accessible by establishing a presence in the students' learning
environment through Blackboard courses.

SHARE MY MUSIC

In a culture where iPods are only slightly less ubiquitous than cell
phones, free and virtually continuous access to music is one of the defining features of the NetGen lifestyle. Music *can* be one of the sharper
wedges dividing generations (and subgroups within generations) into
hostile camps, but music also bridges distances and creates connections
between disparate elements within the culture. The library's extensive
collection of jazz, classical, and popular music CDs, which supports the
academic curriculum *and* individual musical explorations in roughly
equal measure, gives the library a very alluring vehicle for establishing
an image as a diverse and valuable resource–if we can capture the students' attention in the first place. This can represent a challenge, given
that students who visit the CD collection during the course of a tour
often seem surprised that the library has a music collection.

According to the OCLC report on *College Students' Perceptions of
Libraries and Information Resources*, only 60% of college students surveyed responded positively to the statement that the library "Is a place
to get books/videos/music" although 56% recognized that "Libraries
are more suitable than bookstores for . . . Access to music."[1] We're free
and we're legal, but we're not likely to get the opportunity to open up
new avenues of musical discovery–or even achieve some level of recognition as a recreational outlet–unless we can find a way to get on a student's radar screen. The file-sharing capabilities of Apple's iTunes
software–discovered by accident–opened the door for us to start thinking about how we could insinuate ourselves into an environment inhab-
ited almost exclusively by students.[2]

What initially appeared to be a hostile attack on our workstation turned out to be a golden opportunity when the new Mac at the reference desk displayed shared playlists of unknown origin after iTunes was launched. By default, the "Look for shared music" options was checked in the iTunes Preferences file on the new machine, and once the shock of seeing other people's music on a library workstation wore off, the notion that we might be able to capitalize on this in some way began to take shape. If music file sharing–and with it the opportunity to move the whole culture forward by anonymously exposing one's peers to one's own highly refined tastes–represented one of the most sacred tenets of the NetGen creed, shouldn't the library become a player in this cultural and educational exchange? A couple of sources persuaded us that the answer was "yes."

Thanks to Joan Lippincott's chapter in *Educating the Net Generation*[3] with its discussions of who NetGen users are, how and where they learn, and specifically, what libraries have to do to accommodate their needs, the library began to recognize the need to rethink its approach to serving our changing student population. Jenny Levine's *The Shifted Librarian* blog played an equally inspirational role. Levine's thoughts on "Information Shift" describe "how the change from pursuing information to receiving information is and will be affecting libraries." She argues that today's students expect information to flow directly to them via any number of digital technologies and pathways, and librarians have to adapt to that reality if they expect to do a good job in terms of providing services to this group. "I think you have to start meeting these kids' information needs in their world, not yours," she argues. "The library has to become more portable or 'shifted.'"[4]

As a means of gaining access to our NetGen audience, the iTunes software has several irresistible advantages: it is available as a free download from Apple (in both Mac and Windows versions) and it can be used to manage and listen to a wide variety of audio file formats including MP3, Apple Lossless, AIFF, WAV, and AAC. Clicking on the "Share my music" Preferences directs iTunes to make the files–either the entire Library of music files stored on the computer hard drive or specific playlists consisting of selected songs–available to other iTunes users on the campus LAN who have activated the "Look for shared music" option on their machines.

Librarians concerned about copyright issues (and the potential for being raided by the Recording Industry Association of America) will be interested to learn that the iTunes software itself imposes a number of restrictions on the sharing process. Only users on the same LAN or subnet can view and listen to the shared files, which prevents external, unauthorized Internet users from accessing the files. Shared files are streamed for listening but *cannot* be downloaded and saved and therefore cannot be burned to a CD. A given playlist or iTunes library may only be accessed five times in the course of a single day. After that, iTunes displays a message to anyone attempting to access a shared playlist indicating that this limit has been reached and that the listener is welcome to try again later.

While students typically share their music anonymously under the cover of an alias, the library immediately saw the advantage of clearly branding the playlists we shared as a library resource: "Schaffer Library–New Music" or "Schaffer Library–Black History Month," for example. Each playlist consists of several dozen complete songs from a variety of CD titles. We enter the Schaffer Library call number in the iTunes Comments field (although this is an optional display field and users may not necessarily have it turned on). The themed playlists that we've created–organized around events on campus or wider cultural events like Hispanic Heritage Month–encompass areas of the CD collection that we would like to showcase.

For a Safe Zone training session arranged by the office of Student Affairs, we created and shared "Schaffer Library–LGBT Music." According to the National Consortium of Directors of LGBT Resources in Higher Education the aim of programs like Safe Zone is to foster "the development of heterosexual allies has for making the culture of a college or university campus more tolerant towards gay, lesbian, bisexual, and transgender (GLBT) students."[5] The message of the LGBT playlist is that the library supports all types of expression and exploration *and* that we are actively doing collection development in this particular area of music (see Figure 1).

Playlists may be seen as perpetual works-in-progress in that tracks can be added, modified, or deleted over time. To maintain interest, playlists are periodically removed from the shared list of files and replaced by new ones. Generally, it's the music collection development librarian who selects tracks that fit the themes represented in the playlists and undertakes the updating while multi-tasking at the reference desk.

iTunes offers several additional tools we are able to use for promoting our CD collection. The "Create an iMix" capability makes it possible to publish the contents of a playlist on the iTunes Music Store Web site, where it becomes available to anyone who connects to the site. An iMix contains a brief preview of each song in the playlist, as long as the song is available from the iTunes Music Store. (Songs in your playlist

FIGURE 1. LGBT Playlist

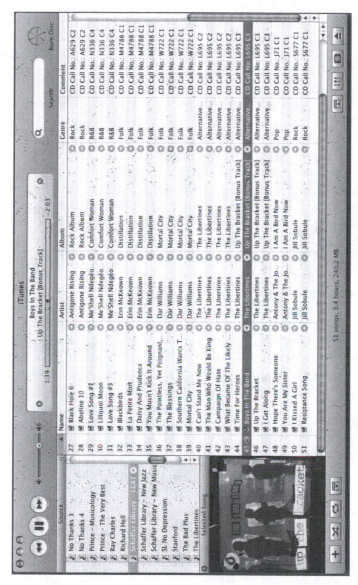

Used with permission.

that are not available for purchase through the Music Store are not listed in the iMix.) Once the iMix is published, clicking on the "Tell a friend" link generates an e-mail notice containing the URL of the iMix that can be sent directly to anyone (on or off campus), or added to any electronic document the library wishes to publish or distribute. An iMix may be edited, revised, renamed, or removed from the Music Store site altogether, making it a very flexible device for marketing the collection.

iTunes Link Maker, an Apple utility designed to facilitate the process of creating a deep link to an artist, CD title, or even the brief sample of a specific song from within the Music Store, is a tool we have used to enhance the catalog record for a CD with links to sound samples, album covers, and biographical and critical material. For some time, we have been operating under the assumption that Amazon is one of the library's chief competitors. If we can engage NetGen library users by emulating–via the library Web OPAC–the experience they have come to expect when they purchase music from an online source, we think we can combat the general perception that libraries and their methods are somehow outdated. The college's recent acceptance into the Apple iTunes appears–as we are coming to understand it–to have the potential to allow us to both expand and stabilize the means of offering access to a range of audio, video, image, and textual file formats.

Are we actually making contact with our students? A modest increase in CD circulation activity is one indication that we are. Just as importantly (given our deeper interest in engaging our community in the CD collection development process) a number of student borrowers have made positive comments to circulation staff on the quality and variety of music that they have discovered in the collection, while others have taken the trouble to recommend specific CD titles for purchase. We do know that library playlists *are* successfully accessed five times a day each, which is the maximum the software permits. That fact, along with the anecdotal evidence from borrowers, suggests that, at the very least, we have managed to infiltrate student-inhabited electronic space and open the lines of communication with those users who are concerned with the quality and content of our CD collection. We hope that if our students look more closely at what we have to offer, that they will see the collection as a diverse and appealing refuge where they can pursue personal tastes and passions in depth and at great length.

OPENING THE LINES OF COMMUNICATION

Opening the lines of communication with online content dates back a decade when Schaffer Library debuted our online newsletter during the Fall of 1996 with Volume 1, Number 1 of "What's New at Schaffer Library." The library building was in the throws of an extensive renovation and expansion project and we needed an avenue with which we could easily communicate and broadcast the daily changes, mess, closings, services, and disruptions that occur when a building is about to be transformed from usable space into a construction zone. If only we were video podcasting then–what entertainment we could have had with a "daily demolition" or "let's see where the books are moving today" series! While we thought it would be beneficial to alert our users to the daily schedule of renovation, we also recognized the need for a medium to disseminate timely news pertaining to resources that might be of interest to students and faculty such as new music, Web sites, databases, research guides, books, and information about people in the library. Our initial Web site also included plans, renderings and drawings for the proposed new building space, as well as recommended readings on the "Information Environment." We printed a hard copy of the first page of the online newsletter near the Reference Desk so students could see what type of content was available, and we promoted the site during library instruction and tours.

Our "What's New at Schaffer" is prominently displayed online and has developed over the years to a very robust Web site (http://www.union.edu/Library/news/whatsnew.htm). Although quite streamlined, it still requires continual maintenance to preserve currency. There is nothing worse then having news that is outdated and inaccurate, especially when we wonder who is really reading this anyway. We realized that if we were to engage our students, we would have to add new material frequently or they might not re-visit.

We began to push timely information out via e-mail, with a link back to the newsletter, so the Union community could get more details if desired. E-mail, of course, creates its own set of problems, and although statistics show that our students are connected socially–with the Internet being the primary communication tool–many students do not use their college accounts and often do not use e-mail at all, relying on text messages and instant messaging. Because we also try to be sensitive to the justifiable concern of annoying students (and faculty) with e-mail bombardment, we always tread lightly when messages are sent, which often leads to the difficult task of selective news coverage. Although we do publish library-related material from time to time in student-centered campus media, this information overload dilemma led us to experiment with blogging and RSS feeds.

The library weblog is simple to update, and we attempt to edit it daily to reflect a new database, film or speaker series, title added, or relevant service interruption. We link from the library home page to the blog as well as to the RSS feed, so students can add this to their newsreader and have our latest "headlines" appear on their desktops. Our blog content usually includes external links to relevant articles and Web sites for additional information. Subject categories are being added, as is easier access to the archive, so students can browse or search by keyword. At present, we still maintain both the online newsletter as well as the blog, but will soon shift our focus towards marketing and expanding our blog presence.

The "blogosphere" is continuing to grow, with a weblog created every second and roughly 16,000 posts every hour, according to blog trackers Technorati (www.technorati.com). Since more students are using social space for communicating and staying connected, there are several advantages in creating blogs, including the fact that students can subscribe if they choose to and we are able to quickly push information out and know that at least a post or two has crossed their horizon. Typically, if we combine this process during the course of an instruction session or through faculty involvement, students will check their e-mail. It is also a way that students can have further input from multiple contributors, as more librarians can easily post messages, news, and recommendations, as opposed to a single Web administrator gathering content from numerous sources. A new library blog space is being designed and ramped up, and we are currently in the process of development that will offer additional customization and end-user options. Branching out from news postings to course-specific information and research guides is a logical next step.

Social software has become popular in library settings, and we are looking to expand from blogs to other forms of social applications such as podcasting, photo and video sharing, social bookmarking, and instant messaging to engage our students.

MEETING STUDENT RESEARCHERS
ON THEIR OWN TERMS

On the academic side, one of our most significant (and risky) initiatives designed to meet NetGen researchers on their own terms involves the library's attempts to engineer a shift from using Google to searching Google Scholar as their primary research tool. This works because Scholar is taught in conjunction with the use of the catalog and of more traditional electronic resources during instructional sessions *and* because we go to some lengths to establish Scholar's dependency upon the library catalog's holdings information and on our subscription resources for delivering the contents of a Google Scholar search.

Thanks to the deep-linking capabilities of OCLC's Open WorldCat and our Serials Solutions link resolver, and based on Schaffer Library's participation in Scholar's "Library Links" program with the display of our customized holdings appearing in search results, Google Scholar has been well received during the course of a typical library instruction session. Google Scholar–with its ability to link directly to articles in resources such as JSTOR and Project Muse–ends up exposing our students to a much wider array of subscription databases than they had previously been aware of (or made use of for research purposes). In fact, use of certain databases increases dramatically after the instruction sessions, so not only does Scholar promote access, but in relationship to what we spend on electronic products, it's an extremely cost-effective marketing tool as well.

Our instructional approach begins with the traditional resources: print and online reference books, the library catalog, and aggregated and subject related databases. Traditionally, in terms of addressing Internet-based research techniques, we were always careful to emphasize the shortcomings inherent in relying solely on Google and other search engines throughout the research process because of the inability to harvest all "hidden Web" data, including peer-reviewed scholarly research. We were equally careful to draw a distinction between materials that are freely available over the Web and those that are *delivered* over the Web, because the library subscribes to resources whose contents are available to our users. Finally, we tend to run searches–and sometimes the same search–in multiple databases in order to call attention to the fact that the coverage in a single database is not exhaustive due to differences in the stated scope of various electronic products. This is a principle that is particularly important to emphasize when teaching Google Scholar given that it only indexes a portion of scholarly material in a wide range of subject areas, and perhaps more significantly, Google has not exactly been forthcoming about what is indexed in Scholar in the first place.

Demonstrations of Google Scholar–typically the last resource we cover in a bibliographic instruction session because we intend to come back to the connection between Scholar and the resources discussed earlier–generally produce a set of useful results that have a number of unique references plus a degree of readily identifiable overlap with the disciplinary and cross-disciplinary databases we have shown to the class. Students react positively to the revelation that the Google they think they know so well is, in reality, a multifaceted resource with (in this case) a valuable component for delivering–thanks to the "Library Links" that have been set up–the sort of scholarly information that will meet with their professor's approval. Searches that end up back in our catalog frequently identify useful book titles that OPAC keyword searches missed because the Google Library project indexes the scanned titles in much more depth than the relatively skeletal keyword terms permit. Similarly, Scholar searches are likely to transport the searcher into the native interface of a subscribed resource. Google Scholar, in other words, will in many instances do a better job of promoting library resources than our own catalog or our carefully designed Web site.

We also employ Google Scholar as an easy introduction to the powerful world of cited reference searching, a feature of Web of Science and Scopus, for example, two resources often times not appropriate for lower-division undergraduate research.

We know from our usage statistics that access to full-text material via Google ranks higher than from many of our other resources and that students generally don't have a clue as to why they have been successfully–or more frustratingly for them–not been successful at article retrieval. Incorporating Google Scholar into our instruction affords us the opportunity to walk students through the library-initiated processes that make some types of information available to them online. Rather then ignore the search engine quandary, we teach students to assess and evaluate their research results, and we feel our students are better able to make informed choices in future research endeavors.

We are aware of issues and controversies associated with advocating the use of Google Scholar in an academic setting. An empirical study in *portal: Libraries and the Academy* analyzes the depth and breadth of Google Scholar in relation to the contents of nearly 50 other databases and uncovers Scholar's relative limitations in terms of currency, uneven humanities and social sciences coverage, and English language bias.[6] Scholar's strengths, the authors demonstrate, include coverage of open access scholarly journals and its potential value as an alternative to much more costly resources for those researchers "who languish in more information-poor environments."

As with any resource, we utilize Scholar when it is most appropriate for the subject matter and certainly take advantage of the strength in coverage. Despite the fact that it is still in beta and therefore a work in progress whose future capabilities are as yet unknown, we have had considerable success with our efforts to introduce Scholar in the reference and instructional settings. From our perspective, Scholar's advantages include:

- Students, who already trust Google implicitly, are not the least bit resistant to embracing a Google product geared toward an academic audience.
- Students not only get useful results, access to full-text, library holdings information, and relevant cited references, but in some instances Scholar produces better results with less effort than searching professional-level resources.
- Many newer faculty members–particularly in the humanities and social sciences–arrive at Union with interdisciplinary specializations and so the encompassing nature of Scholar suits the researcher and teacher whose work and classroom assignments span multi-disciplinary boundaries.
- In similar fashion, many Union faculty are designing courses and doing research that crosses divisional lines–artists are working with biologists, physicists with musicians, historians with engineers, ethicists with economists–and here, too, Scholar's holistic, "adisciplinary" nature means a researcher does not have to know the appropriate database(s), journal(s), or literature in order to plunge into the process of retrieving useful references and full-text articles.

Our experiences with a history seminar on Italian fascism–where we individually introduced two dozen students to Scholar and a range of other relevant history resources–served very nicely as a lab for observing Google Scholar in action. Students were scheduled to meet with a reference librarian for a one-on-one consultation. All arrived with a previously approved research topic, which ranged from the more "purely" historical (the role of the *squadrismo*, relations with Italy's North African colonies, fascism and the Jews) to research projects that took a somewhat more interdisciplinary approach (such as fascism and sports, women, philosophy, film, military technology, and art). Many had done at least a little preliminary research in the library catalog and online, most commonly in JSTOR.

We started in the catalog as a way of getting acquainted with the appropriate keyword and Library of Congress subject heading terminology, referring as needed to a couple of relevant historical dictionaries for clarification and to discover any potential alternate search terms. Searches in the catalog were typically exported in two directions–into ProQuest and EBSCOhost via the WebBridge feature of the Innovative Interfaces ILS and into the union catalog of the ConnectNY system via the Innovative INN-Reach software which facilitates direct, patron-initiated borrowing from participating libraries. For most students, these tasks generally went beyond their previous library experience.

From there we searched *Historical Abstracts*, refining our strategies to include only English-language materials since there were no speakers of Italian in this group. We explained the concept of a bibliographic database (in response to a NetGen student who asked "So what's the point?") and demonstrated *Historical Abstracts'* limited linking and catalog look-up capabilities. In each case, however, results were surprisingly disappointing with few useful references produced no matter how the search was revised. Duty done, we turned finally to Google Scholar.

We intentionally went first to Google in order to talk about why college faculty are dubious about student's using this as their primary research tool. At the basic Google search page, we clicked on the Scholar link, which (Web designers take note) most of the students had never noticed or used. Here was our opportunity to portray Scholar as Google's response to the criticism regarding the absence of peer review, and therefore from a scholarly perspective, the questionable authority of the information found using the search engine. This was also the time to point out that a Scholar search, in fact, would return results from peer-reviewed scholarly journals and from academic press. We noted Scholar's status as a beta product and switched to the Advanced Scholar Search mode, where we ran the search strategy for the student's research topic, generally with the "Social Sciences, Arts, and Humanities" box checked in the Subject Areas section of the interface.

Google Scholar, for every topic, produced better results than *Historical Abstracts*. Scholar cut across boundaries to produce a more extensive listing of articles and uncovered in most cases a useful listing of cited references for further exploration. The process of scanning scholarly books for the Google Libraries project gave the students a much deeper look between the covers of the academic press books in the database, frequently turning up useful titles from our own collection that had been missed by the process of keyword searching in our own catalog.

We pointed out that the "Full-Text @ My Library" link indicated that a particular article was available online and employed this opportunity to reiterate how this access was made possible because the library subscribed to a resource that held the rights to publish the article electronically. We also explained that someone who did the exact same Scholar search but was not from Union College might not be able to access the full text of most of the articles in the results list because, again, that was dependent upon the library's subscription to various electronic resources. We pursued several links, producing full-text of the article plus access to the native electronic subscription resources, which were then available for additional searching if the student chose to do so (see Figure 2).

Finally we clicked on the "Library Search" link, called attention to the fact that Scholar recognized that we were initiating the search from Union College, and selected the "Search the catalog at Schaffer Library" link where the student discovered either that the library owned the title or that we could extend the search to the ConnectNY system where it could be easily requested (see Figure 2). In summary, our approach to teaching Scholar begins with establishing the value of the catalog and the databases, proceeds to the specifics of accessing and searching Scholar itself, and then circles back to the resources that form the library-dependent foundation of Scholar's full text, library holdings, and document delivery functions.

In contrast, instruction in the more formal classroom setting generally does not permit us to focus so directly and extensively on the research needs of a single individual in the way that these consultations allowed. Here we have devised a strategy that enables us to both follow up on the instructional session *and* make individual contact. Like most librarians, we feel somewhat compelled to create a handout that depicts search strategies employed during the session and recalls the resources that we demonstrated. Rather than pass it out in the session, though, or post it on the library Web site where it may never be visited again once the session ends, our current practice is to announce during the session that students will shortly be receiving a handout by e-mail. We allow several days to pass and then send the handout in Microsoft Word or PDF format directly to each student's e-mail account. This works because librarians (and faculty) have access to students' campus e-mail addresses via the online class rosters (see Figure 3).

The handouts we disseminate make use of Word and Acrobat's ability to embed hyperlinks to the sources within the documents and display screen shots that are incorporated into the handout. This e-mail message offers additional assistance to the students in the class, reinforces the

FIGURE 2. Google Scholar Search

Google Scholar results are linked to our library's online catalog via Open WorldCat

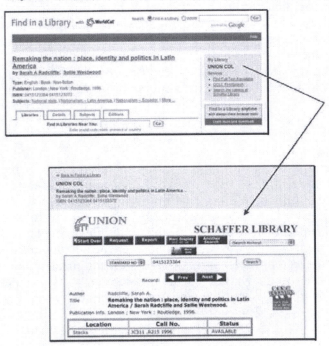

Used with permission.

material covered in the session, gives the students a tool that allows them to go directly to any of the resources we discussed in class, and creates a direct link back to the librarian who conducted the session. It also gives the faculty member something that he or she can later employ when consulting with a student on a research project. Typically, the e-

FIGURE 3. Email to Students

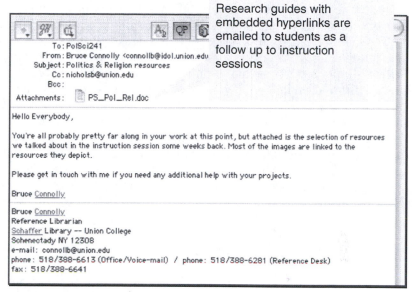

Research guides with embedded hyperlinks are emailed to students as a follow up to instruction sessions

Used with permission.

mailed handout produces questions or a request for an appointment with a librarian from students who attended the session.

MAKING LIBRARIANS MORE VISIBLE

Our involvement with Union's Blackboard site and embedding librarians within courses is also another way of connecting and collaborating in online communities with our students and faculty. By placing librarians in our students' learning environment we are much more visible and reachable. Our teaching faculty can add contact information for a specific librarian or add a librarian as a course builder or teaching assistant to a Blackboard page. This allows us to monitor or hold "reference hours" via e-mail chats or discussion boards before and after instruction, and be conveniently available for additional research questions throughout the term. Custom Web sites and handouts are typically created for our library instruction sessions, so our accessibility through Blackboard alleviates the necessity of students monitoring their Blackboard courses, while at the same time examining a peripheral set of instructions and resources from the library. Library material is conveniently placed within the course as an integral part of the class, helping students to learn in a context of use for completing assignments.

Union's acceptance into Apple's iTunes University program provides us with another potential avenue for reaching the NetGen population. While based on Apple's popular iTunes Music Store, the company is marketing iTunes University as a content management system (as opposed to simply a music acquisition system) capable of delivering all kinds of information in a wide variety of file formats. We will be interested to see how faculty put this to work, but are also intrigued by the relative openness of iTunes U, which unlike Blackboard, does not require a student (or librarian) to be registered in a specific course in order to have access to materials stored in iTunes. This approach means the librarians may not need to be quite so dependent on faculty when it comes to getting valuable course-related research materials directly into the hands of students.

THE MESSAGE

What does it say about the Library that we are exploring multiple approaches toward making direct contact with our students? Actually, it would probably say more about us, and say it in a very unflattering way, if we neglected this opportunity.

Increasingly, public and school libraries are offering applications and services, collectively known as "Web 2.0," where users can share content and easily collaborate with others through the use of wikis, blogs and podcasts. Public libraries especially are reaching out to teens by offering RSS feeds to deliver digital content for new books, summer reading lists and reviews. Many public libraries currently offer library blogs, Flickr spaces, and library MySpace profiles for teen patrons. Podcasts and vodcasts created through partnerships with public and school libraries that deliver audio book reviews, research instruction, summer readings, and book talks are proliferating as well.

Not surprisingly, incoming first-year students entering our learning environment arrive expecting these kinds of services and technologies to be part of the academic picture that we present. On their behalf, Joan Lippincott asks: "Why should libraries and librarians adapt their well-structured organizations and systems to the needs of students rather than insist that students learn about and adapt to existing library systems?"[7] The answer, from our perspective, is that all the approaches that we've taken–music file sharing, opening the lines of communication through a variety of technological avenues, engineering a painless shift from a standard search engine to one geared specifically to academic needs and expectations, and finally, taking the step of personally becoming a presence in the NetGen cybercultural realm–all of these together serve as a clear statement testifying to the library's willingness to meet them in a familiar, comfortable, and vibrant space of their choosing and that we are just as eager to invite them into our space if they choose to come.

Not all of our students are technologically adept, and it's a balancing act to maintain a welcoming atmosphere for the digital stragglers without being relegated to the sidelines by the more adventurous NetGen explorer. We hope our attempts to bridge the cultural divide will not only engage our students, but will also expand the possibilities of direct interaction. As Marc Prensky states when discussing technology in his essay "Adopt and Adapt" in *Edutopia*: "Let's adapt it, push it, pull it, iterate with it, experiment with it, test it, and redo it,"[8] and that is what we are aiming to do. The library, its electronic resources, and its service ethic are all so inextricably linked and so indistinguishable from one another at this point, that it no longer makes much sense to think of marketing any single aspect of what we do in isolation from the others.

REFERENCES

1. *College Students' Perceptions of Libraries and Information Resources: A Report to the OCLC Membership.* (Dublin, Ohio: OCLC Online Computer Library Center, Inc., 2006).

2. Bruce Connolly, "Promoting the Library's CD Collection via iTunes File Sharing," *Computers in Libraries* (November/December 2005): 25, no. 10, 6-8, 53-56.

3. Joan Lippincott, "Net Generation Students and Libraries," in *Educating the Net Generation*, eds. Diana G. Oblinger and James L. Oblinger, (Boulder, Colorado: EDUCAUSE, 2005). Available electronically at <http://www.educause.edu/educatingthenetgen/>.

4. Jenny Levine. "What is a Shifted Librarian?" *The Shifted Librarian*, 20 May 2004, http://www.theshiftedlibrarian.com/stories/2002/01/19/hatIsAShiftedLibrarian.html (19 July 2006).

5. National Consortium of Directors of LGBT Resources in Higher Education, "Frequently Asked Questions," 2005, <http://www.lgbtcampus.org/faq/safe_zone.html> (19 July 2006).

6. Chris Neuhaus, Ellen Neuhaus, Alan Asher, and Clint Wrede, "The Depth and Breadth of Google Scholar: An Empirical Study," *portal: Libraries and the Academy*, (April 2006): 6, no. 2, 127-141.

7. Joan Lippincott, "Net Generation Students and Libraries," in *Educating the Net Generation.* (EDUCAUSE, 2005), 13.12.

8. Marc Prensky, "Adopt and Adapt," *Edutopia* (December/January 2006), 42-45.

Using RSS Feeds to Alert Users to Electronic Resources

Kim Armstrong

INTRODUCTION

The "orange button" now present on so many commercial Web sites, ranging from news (BBC, Reuters, CBS News) to blogs, is also gaining a presence on library Web sites as a way to keep library users informed about new acquisitions, digital content, electronic resources, and library events. "Really Simple Syndication," aka "RDF Site Summary," aka "Rich Site Summary," is a recent technology. RSS is an XML-based format that allows the sharing of Web site content. RSS feeds give frequent users of Web sites a streamlined and efficient mechanism for tracking updates without making individual visits to dozens or hundreds of Web sites.

In the 2005 publication "Perceptions of Libraries and Information Resources: a Report to the OCLC Membership," 3,348 people took part in a survey of information-seeking behaviors.[1] The findings reported that eighty-four percent of those surveyed use non-proprietary search engines to begin an information search and that only one percent begin their search on a library Web site. This survey reveals the need for aggressive marketing of the electronic resources in which libraries have invested heavily and that provide quality and trustworthy information to users. Libraries continue to experiment with the concept of meeting patrons where they are, by offering services through e-mail, chat, and via social network sites such as Facebook.com and Myspace.com.

ADVANTAGES OF USING PUSH TECHNOLOGY TO MAKE USERS AWARE OF E-RESOURCES

Wikipedia defines push technology as "an Internet-based content delivery system where information is delivered from a central server to a client computer based upon a predefined set of request parameters outlined by the client computer. Push Technology differs from normal Internet technology, which is based on Pull Technology where a user has to request a Web site through an internet browser." The entry goes on to say that "push technology became the acronym–RSS."[2]

Increasingly, libraries recognize that users are not as likely to come into a physical space to learn about new products and services, nor are they likely to begin content searches from the libraries' Web site. Additionally, many libraries serve users in remote locations who will never interact with the library except through technological delivery of content and services. As libraries commit larger and larger portions of their materials budgets to electronic content, it is critical that they also design ways to inform users that these resources exist for their use.

Libraries no longer have the level of control over access to information that existed in the past. We are in competition with worldwide, 24/7 content providers who capture our users' time and attention via simple searching, ease of use, and accessibility. If we are to succeed in providing quality information in a convenient, timely, and efficient manner to our users, we must appear in their information space and not wait for them to discover us as a separate resource, disintegrated, and disengaged from their information discovery sources. As libraries, we can use RSS feeds to distribute news, messages, and announcements to our users that will not be lost in e-mails, filters, or become recycled newsletters.

The availability of RSS feeds from library Web sites has increased over the past few years, but most often the feeds are for the purpose of advertising library programming rather than the acquisition of new resources. In a May 2006 review of Web sites of the members of the Association of Research Libraries, the leading 123 North American research institutions, only fifteen offered an RSS feed from their library's homepage. Many more of the ARL members offer RSS feeds from other sections of the Web site, but patrons have to look well beyond the main page to discover them. There are a number of good articles that describe how individual libraries managed the process of setting up feeds.[3]

Libraries planning to offer RSS feeds may find it necessary to provide instructions to setup an account for an RSS reader or news aggregator as a first step. Unlike many other Web services though, RSS readers are generally free and do not require individuals to provide personal information, e-mail addresses, or logins. Since he patron controls the sites from which they want to draw content, no spam or false hits will creep into their accounts. Some libraries have posted a quick tutorial on how to setup an RSS reader. The MIT Libraries' "RSS: Keeping Up with Research"[4] and Northwestern University's "How to Use RSS Feeds"[5] are good examples.

RSS readers can be accessed via XML compatible devices such as desktop computers, handheld devices such as Palm Pilots, Treo, pagers, BlackBerry, and others. Some of the popular and available free or feebased aggregators for news feeds are Bloglines, UserLand, Pluck, and my Yahoo. The Web site RSSFeeds.com <http://www.rssfeeds.com> lists RSS readers to choose based on costs, additional functionality, and feed format.

Patrons who establish an account for an RSS reader, either via the Web, or by downloading reader software, will then have the tools to manage large amounts of information from disparate content providers. They will be able to stay current without having to visit individual Web sites for new information. Users will save time because they can customize their RSS accounts to give them brief headers of information each time a Web site is updated and the user can view their aggregated RSS content at the time and place that they prefer. RSS feeds are popular for frequent bloggers because they can be notified each time someone adds a new entry to a blog.

EXAMPLES OF LIBRARIES' USE OF RSS

Gerry McKiernan at the Iowa State University Library maintains several registries of library-related RSS feeds. His "RSS(sm): Rich Site Services"[6] is a listing of selected feeds from public and academic libraries, publishers, newspapers, and relevant Web sites. The feeds are organized by categories such as: cataloging, databases, instruction, new books, and reference services. This site gives any library considering the publication of its Web content an overview of the possible function of an RSS feed and good examples of Web sites designed to deliver feeds.

LISFeeds.com, maintained by Blake Carver and Steven M. Cohen, aggregates global library related content from hundreds of sites.[7] Most of the feeds are in English, but there are also Spanish and German postings. In contrast to RSS(sm), LISFeeds contains fewer library feeds and many more individual blogs alongside feeds from the American Library Association and OCLC.

Many libraries offer an all-in-one RSS feed. The content of these feeds covers a variety of topics that might include library events, new book lists, branch library news, recent gifts, and changes to library hours. In a digital environment in which users can manipulate and design information tailored to their specific needs, this approach can be too general. Increasingly, academic libraries are offering users a menu of RSS feeds to match their interests. The examples below illustrate the diversity of electronic resources now available to library users and the unique feeds being used to promote them.

The University of Tennessee Libraries offers an "Electronic Resources News" feed for current information about databases, electronic journals, ebooks, and digital images. The Web page created for e-resource news also includes links to feeds on more general library topics, such as SciTech and Music and scholarly communication.[8]

The University of Oklahoma Libraries makes their LORA (Library Online Resources Access) news available via an RSS feed. As new databases and electronic content are added, subscribers to the feed will be notified. The entries for new electronic resources that are published for RSS readers are concise and brief so the users can quickly scan the entries.[9]

The Australian National University provides new title lists of items recently cataloged in their Innovative Library system. Not all of the materials, though, are print resources. Subscribers to the "New Serial Titles" feed will find many individual electronic journals that are being cataloged and added to the library collection.[10]

The University of North Carolina at Chapel Hill highlights its digital collection, "Documenting the American South," through a unique RSS feed. Subscribers will learn about additions to the southern history collection, which includes primary sources such as diaries, letters, oral history interviews, and books.[11]

An RSS feed will notify individuals when a new paper has been placed into the "e-scholarship" institutional repository hosted by the California Digital Library. The repository is a free, open access tool that allows the public the opportunity to read the scholarly output of the departments, centers, and research units throughout the University of California system.[12]

The University of Maryland, Baltimore County extends the traditional notion of library electronic resources by offering an RSS feed for their streaming media collection. Many libraries and other units on campus, particularly those involved in distance or online learning, are beginning to build collections of commercially available streaming content to replace physical videocassettes and DVDs. Users will also discover a wealth of locally created lectures, films, and music performances that can be linked to through the RSS feed and viewed freely when the university holds the permissions.[13]

SUGGESTIONS FOR OTHER RSS SITES
(PUBLISHERS, JOURNAL AGGREGATORS)

Researchers will also discover that RSS feeds are now available from many publishers and content aggregators to provide customized information based on a user's research or topical interests. Just as in the recent past when libraries provided Table of Contents alert services (TOCs), RSS feeds can expand the research services available to the individual. At the same time that libraries promote new electronic resources via their feeds, they can also inform users that direct feeds may be available from the publisher or aggregator site with additional customization alternatives.

The May 9, 2006 *USA Today* newspaper ran an article entitled "RSS feeds college student's diet for research."[14] The author describes how an undergraduate at the University of Pennsylvania uses RSS feeds to quickly scan contents from dozens of Web sites to select appropriate content for assignments. The point is made that "running searches on Google or Yahoo! will bring back so many irrelevant sources." Using RSS, users can pre-select trusted content sites and add them to their aggregated sources so that they don't have to spend more time evaluating accuracy, relevancy, or credibility of the source material.

Several content providers and aggregators provide users with RSS feed options. EBSCOhost offers an RSS feed service for users who setup profiles for journal TOC alerts and for the results of saved searches. Users can control the frequency of the search to be run against the EBSCO databases (daily, weekly, monthly). The results of database searches can be refined to include only the most recent articles or articles published within specific timeframes.

Project Muse offers feeds for latest journal issues, news, updates, and title additions to the Muse collections. Subscribers will have direct access to the full-text articles from the RSS feeds. Sage Publishers uses RSS feeds to provide alerting services for table of contents, keyword, author, and citation alerts.

Science publishers from the for-profit, society, and open access communities have had quick uptake of RSS feeds and are adding rich metadata to their notifications. Nature Publishing not only covers its journal content via feeds, but makes job openings and scientific news announcements available. The American Chemical Society has feeds that let users know immediately when an article is posted to the Web, which eliminates the wait traditionally tied to the publication of a journal issue. BioMed Central users can access the latest articles, a list of the most-viewed articles in the last 30 days, and the Faculty of 1000 "hidden jewels."

Libraries can combine their announcements of new electronic resources with information about feeds directly available from the provider of the electronic resource. This powerful combination offers users a direct connection to quality resources without having to search through Web sites or endure static descriptions or lengthy tutorials. For example, the Engineering Resources Blog from the Drexel University Libraries offers an RSS feed to keep users informed of new print and electronic resources for engineering and biomedical engineering. The announcements of newly available resources also include information about feeds available directly from the resource provider.[15]

RSS TECHNOLOGY AND TOOLS NEEDED
TO IMPLEMENT FEEDS FROM LIBRARY WEB SITES

There are many fine Web sites, guides, and articles available that describe the technical processes for libraries to create and publish RSS feeds. Gerry McKiernan's RSS(sm) site has an extensive bibliography available that includes primers and tutorials for content publishers (libraries) and Web or technology staff.[16]

A library's first step in implementing an RSS feed is to decide on the version of RSS that is to be used for publishing content. Currently, there is no standard for RSS, and there are several versions that are widely used. Most RSS readers will accommodate and support feeds from all of the available versions (RSS 0.91, RSS 1.0, RSS 2.0). Then the library creates a description of the content it wants to publicize or distribute in an XML-based format. Many content providers register their RSS with a directory such as Syndic8 (http://www.syndic8.com/). Most libraries will find it sufficient to provide a link or multiple links on their Web sites that users can click on to add to their selected aggregator for collecting and reading feeds.

For additional help to create a usable and effective RSS feed, Paul Miller's article in *Ariadne*, "Syndicated content, it's more than just some file formats," presents a wonderful list of guidelines for good practice in the use of RSS. [17] Ken Varnum, a librarian at Tufts University, is the author of RSS4Lib. It is a weblog of innovative ways libraries use RSS.[18]

Libraries that have well-organized Web sites and that already have added "What's New" or "Update" sections to their pages will be able to migrate their work quite easily over to an RSS feed. The technologies are already in place and widely used, and there are many good examples to draw upon. The tutorials, manuals, and books available on the topic should help any staff member familiar enough with technology to participate in Web site development and to take the next step to market the library's resources. The appetite for readily available access and the presence of ubiquitous networking have spurred libraries to invest heavily in e-content. Promoting that content via RSS is a crucial step for user discovery and use.

CONCLUSION

The growth of electronic resources that are being licensed, purchased, and even developed and hosted by libraries offers the library user a wealth of information previously unavailable to anyone not willing to visit the physical library location. Library professionals are encouraging publishers to digitize journal backruns and books.

However, libraries have learned that they are in competition with freely available Web sites and search engines for their user's attention. While the electronic resources that are selected and paid for by the library may clearly be more credible and authoritative, studies of Internet use behavior proves that our elaborate structures and information systems may be too difficult to navigate by comparison. In OCLC's "Perceptions" report, seventy-two percent of respondents had used a search engine on the Internet, sixteen percent had searched an online library database.[19]

Guiding users to quality resources has always been an important function for librarians, but the task is becoming more and more difficult. Rather than waiting for individuals to come to our libraries or to seek out our Web sites with recommendations and annotations, we can make the discovery of resources convenient and simple.

The adoption of RSS feeds to inform users about electronic resources gives the library a fairly simple and inexpensive opportunity to reach users at their convenience. Because many commercial Web sites have been using RSS longer than the educational community, users will already be familiar with the orange button and the implied service that it offers. The opportunity for the library to present news and information that is shaped and collected according to the user's interest is critical if we are to effectively reach our target audience.[20]

NOTES

1. OCLC, "Perceptions of Libraries and Information Resources: a Report to the OCLC Membership," http://www.oclc.org/reports/pdfs/Percept_all.pdf (accessed October 16, 2006).

2. Wikipedia contributors, "Push Technology," *Wikipedia, The Free Encyclopedia*, http://en.wikipedia.org/wiki/Push_technology (accessed October 16, 2006).

3. Zhu, Qin. "The nuts and bolts of delivering new technical reports via database-generated RSS feeds." *Computers in Libraries* (February 2006): 24-28.

4. MIT. 2006. "RSS: Keeping Up with Research," http://libraries.mit.edu/help/rss/ (accessed October 16, 2006).

5. Northwestern University Library. 2005. "How to use RSS Feeds," http://www.library.northwestern.edu/rssinfo.html (accessed October 16, 2006).

6. McKiernan, Gerry. 2004. "RSS(sm): Rich Site Services," http://www.public.iastate.edu/~CYBERSTACKS/RSS.htm (accessed October 16, 2006).

7. Carver, Blake and Steven M. Cohen. "Librarian RSS Feeds," http://lisfeeds.com/ (accessed October 16, 2006).

8. The University of Tennessee Libraries. 2005. "Electronic Resources News," http://www.lib.utk.edu/news/eres/ (accessed October 16, 2006).

9. The University of Oklahoma Libraries. 2006. "University Libraries RSS Feeds," http://libraries.ou.edu/rss/ (accessed October 16, 2006).

10. The Australian National University Library. 2005. "New Title Lists: RSS Feeds," http://anulib.anu.edu.au/epubs/innopacnewbooksrss.html (accessed October 16, 2006).

11. The University Library. The University of North Carolina at Chapel Hill. 2005. "News and Events," http://www.lib.unc.edu/rss/index.html (accessed October 16, 2006).

12. California Digital Library. 2006. "eScholarship," http://repositories.cdlib.org/escholarship/ (accessed October 16, 2006).

13. New Media Studio. University of Maryland Baltimore County. 2006. "Streaming Media@UMBC," http://asp1.umbc.edu/newmedia/studio/stream/index.cfm (accessed October 16, 2006).

14. Ly, Anh. 2006. "RSS Feeds College Students Diet for Research." *USATODAY.com*, August 1, 2005. http://www.usatoday.com/tech/news/2005-08-01-rss-research_x.htm (accessed October 16, 2006).

15. Drexel University Libraries. 2006. "Engineering Resources." http://englibrary.blogspot.com/ (accessed October 16, 2006).

16. McKiernan, Gerry. 2005. "RSS(SM): Rich Site Services. General Bibliography," http://www.public.iastate.edu/~CYBERSTACKS/GenBib.htm (accessed October 16, 2006).

17. Miller, Paul. 2003. "Syndicated content: it's more than just some file formats?" *Ariadne*, no. 35. http://www.ariadne.ac.uk/issue35/miller/intro.htm (accessed October 16, 2006).

18. Varnum, Ken. 2006. "RSS4Lib: Innovative Ways Libraries Use RSS," http://www.rss4lib.com/ (accessed October 16, 2006).

19. OCLC, "Perceptions of Libraries and Information Resources: a Report to the OCLC Membership," http://www.oclc.org/reports/pdfs/Percept_all.pdf (accessed October 16, 2006).

20. Byrne, Gillian. "RSS and Libraries-Fad or the Future?" *Feliciter* 2 (2005): 62-63.

Referral Marketing Campaigns: "Slashdotting" Electronic Resources

James Buczynski

Libraries' information consumer market share continues to freefall despite the opportunities that have emerged with the arrival of the Information Age. We've built digital libraries, offering access to immense digital collections of quality resources, and online service desks staffed by skilled experts, but the crowds are not coming. Marketing missteps are largely to blame for the declining role of libraries in people's lives. There is an awareness gap between the offering of digital libraries and the communities they serve. Word-of-mouth (WOM), or referral marketing, is proposed as a bridge to span this awareness gap. Blogs and online social networking services aggregate listeners, enabling WOM marketers to reach more people than has ever been possible before using existing marketing channels. The following chapter outlines WOM marketing in a library context, addressing library specific challenges and opportunities.

THE CHALLENGE OF MARKETING DIGITAL LIBRARIES: COMPETITION AND POSITIONING

In the early 1990s, libraries lost their distribution oligopoly on freely available information. Freely available, based on the perspective of library patrons–obviously the library was directly supported by the community they served through taxes and often membership fees. In less than a decade, the ubiquitous adoption of the Internet as a content and communication medium created a new competitive environment for libraries. In this new environment, the old practice of "build it and they will come" no longer holds true. There are too many options in the online content marketplace. Digital libraries don't stand out in the universe of online information. Search and retrieval intermediaries, like library reference staff, are no longer vital for searching success. Searchers self-serve. Libraries built digital collections, deployed online realtime research assistance service points, but the crowds are not coming.

A review of library-related literature suggests there is no consensus about how far libraries' information consumer market share has fallen since the emergence of the Internet. Intuitively, it will vary by sector (public, academic, corporate, government, etc.) and will be heavily correlated to long-term funding trends. Everyone talks about "the problem," but few studies go beyond anecdotal evidence to empirical evidence. *Service Trends in ARL Libraries, 1991-2004* is widely quoted as proof that reference service transactions have fallen across academic research libraries.[1] A 34% drop in reference service transactions was reported by the longitudinal library service study.

Recently, OCLC's *Perceptions of Libraries and Information Resources* study confirmed that digital libraries have a limited or nonexistent role in people's lives today.[2] The study's respondents reported that they are using libraries less and less since the Internet emerged. Of those queried, 84% of the respondents began their search process by accessing a Web search engine, compared to 1% that began with the library's Web site. The library's resources are increasingly less visible to today's information consumers. They are not aware of what is available in libraries: 58% did not know libraries offered full-text content like e-journals and databases; 33% did not know the library had a Web site. Libraries as a "brand" were found to be synonymous with books. Librarians know that for today's information consumer if it's not online, it does not exist. No wonder libraries were reported to be the last place many people go looking for information. Libraries have an image problem.

Declining or stagnant customer bases don't bode well for continued library funding. Viewed at the simplest level as an expenditure, libraries are constantly a target for budget cuts by municipalities, corporations, institutions, and schools. Whereas resource borrowing/circulation and library visitor volume were the old library currency for securing funding, page views and resource downloads are the new currency. In this new environment, libraries are competing for traffic with a constantly growing list of competitors, many of which are considerably better funded. The stakes are high. The OCLC study suggests that marketing missteps are largely to blame for the declining role of libraries in people's lives. Most information consumers are not aware of the digital collections available to them from their library—be it in a corporate, educational or municipal setting. There is an awareness gap between the holdings of digital libraries and the communities they serve.

MARKETING THE LIBRARY vs. MARKETING ITS SPECIFIC RESOURCES

Marketing is a means of ensuring that libraries, librarians, and librarianship are integrated into both today's and tomorrow's emerging global culture.[3] It is a process for linking products, services, results and roles. Unfortunately, digital libraries are not easy to market because it is difficult to communicate what they are about. The World Wide Web is perceived as a "global digital library"–offering fee and free e-books, e-journals, online images, and sound recording or video archives. Everyone's in the business of organizing access to online resources. Differentiation from competitors is increasingly difficult.

There is a long tradition of marketing libraries as "places." Campaigns aim to bring more people to the library, to use its services and facilities, and to increase borrowing and visitor statistics. Libraries are marketed as places of solitude, learning, leisure, business, and assistance. Available facilities and resources holdings are often highlighted in community marketing campaigns. The same marketing mindset has been applied to the marketing of digital library collections and services. The focus of campaigns has been on building awareness about a library's Web site, the library's "place," so to speak, in today's online information universe. We've advertised the URL, embedded it in various relevant community Web sites (homepages of high schools, colleges, universities, corporate intranets, etc.), assuming if people know the URL, they'll come. Once inside, they'll see all the amazing resources and search tools available.

Focusing on marketing the digital library as a place both similar and complimentary to the physical library has not resonated with patrons. By trying to promote everything, they are in fact promoting nothing. Vague, all-encompassing marketing messages are tuned out by listeners. Libraries are still trying to bring traffic through the front door (its Web site), in an environment where searchers expect direct access to resources. Libraries are still using that "come over to my place," come visit "my portal," mindset. Use any Web search engine, or file sharing network, and you'll find resources that are directly accessible. You don't have to go to the home page first, or some listing of Web site contents; instead you pull up the resource directly. If you cannot, you hit the 'back button." This holds true whether you are clicking on a hyperlink in a blog entry, community of shared interest portal or a results list from a search engine. The challenge for libraries is how to integrate their digital resources into the Web sites frequented by their users. In essence, it is a product placement challenge.

Product placement, targeted to a library's user groups, is inherently difficult in the online universe. There are too many options for placement; Web sites rapidly rise and fall in popularity. A recent study in *Behaviour and Information Technology Journal* suggests online viewers are more fickle than we thought.[4] The study found that people make judgments about a Web page in one-twentieth of a second, less than half the time it takes to blink. The first impression evoked by a page matters. Everyone is chasing the online crowds. Whoever has them is inundated with requests for advertising space on the site. Fee or free, the competition is fierce. Staying on top of who is hot and who is not, is extremely time-consuming and may not even be sustainable.

The Internet is open to all by design, yet some of a given digital library's resources may be available to all seekers while others have access technologically limited to a library's user groups. Partnering with externals is restricted by this contradiction. A library cannot limit product placement to Web sites hosted by the library's funding body. A library's online user base extends well beyond their funding body's online space. Product placement in the library's physical space is ineffective, given the trend that fewer people are visiting physical libraries, and less often.[5] Word-of-mouth (WOM) marketing of a digital library's resources is the most promising marketing solution to the challenge of marketing a library's digital holdings in today's information consumer marketplace. Technology-mediated WOM marketing delivers the results libraries have been seeking for so long.

THE POWER OF WORD OF MOUTH (WOM) MARKETING

WOM, referral or "viral" marketing, is not new. The ideas and practices have been around for a long time. The part that is new is the reach that today's technology gives it.[6] WOM is a form of interpersonal communication among consumers concerning their personal experiences with a firm, service or a product.[7] Bone defines it best as an "exchange of comments, thoughts and ideas among two or more individuals in which none of the individuals represents the marketing source."[8] Techniques are used to exploit pre-existing social networks. WOM marketing takes place within a context of everyday, routine, relational interactions.[9] By human nature, people praise products that work for them.[10] In essence, conversation is used as a marketing tool. Datta, Chowdhury and Chakraborty[11] and Silverman[12] provide a great survey of the literature. The Word of Mouth Marketing Association's <http://www.womma.org/index.htm> annual conference is great source of current trade practices and case studies.

As the information universe continues to inundate people with options, it is harder to reach people with messages.[13] Advertising is becoming less and less effective.[14] People have always used social networks as a starting point to get information, which is why WOM marketing is thousands of times as powerful as conventional marketing.[15] Testimonials and endorsements by experts or peers can rapidly produce exponential increases in brand awareness both in terms of a message's visibility and effect.[16] The biggest e-commerce players (Amazon, Google, etc.), media archives (Flickr, YouTube, etc.) and social networking sites (Facebook, MySpace, etc.) don't market for success–they use WOM to spread awareness.[17] WOM is what drives the online crowds to your portal or content. Slashdot <http://slashdot.org/> showed the world in 1997 how powerful electronically mediated conversations could be in terms of directing traffic to little-known Web sites.

People find great Web sites by sampling their content from other known Web sites. Online traffic follows "referrals" to specific resources held at specific online providers. It is known as the "Slashdot effect." Slashdot is a popular technology news and information site that is updated many times daily with articles that are short summaries of stories on other websites with links to the stories. Slashdot is known for directing huge volumes of internet traffic to small unknown Web sites, causing the servers on which they are hosted to crash. People say you've been Slashdotted, when a listing on one Web site causes traffic to spike on your Web site. As Slashdot and other Web sites have demonstrated over time, referrals, especially those populated by community members, are key to marketing in an information marketplace saturated with options. Traffic flows from popular Web sites and portals to other connected sites.

WOM IN THE ONLINE WORLD:
BLOGS, SOCIAL NETWORKS, PODCASTS, WEB SITES, CONTENT SYSTEMS, AND LISTSERVS

The online masses are not only consumers of information and content, they are producers too. Each year it becomes easier and easier to create and disseminate content online. Computing hardware and software and hosting services are emerging to continually lower the barriers to becoming a provider in the online content marketplace. While in the early 1990s, technology skill sets were required to participate, today anyone with basic word processing and Web browsing experience can have a voice online. That voice has a potential for tremendous reach. OCLC's *Perceptions of Libraries and Information Resources* study found that 59% of respondents use recommendations from a trusted source.[18] Although product and service referrals are prone to abuse, Terveen,[19] David,[20] and Hassan[21] argue that reputation management is a strong deterrent to mischief and dishonest referrals in online settings. It is easy to be ostracized from your online communities.

Blogs, social networks, podcasts, Web sites, content systems and listservs serve as the infrastructure supporting today's global conversations about any topic imaginable. Each has its individual characteristics:

- Blogs are reverse chronological, online diaries supported by simple, easy-to-use publishing software. Technorati <http://www.technorati.com/>, a blog directory, tracks over 45 million blogs. In 2005, the Pew Internet & American Life Project found that 7% of U.S. adults blog, 27% read them and 12% have commented on blog postings.[22] Bloggers and their readers tend to be early adopters of products and services.[23]
- Internet social networks are online services that provide social connection infrastructure using multiple communication channels (web, IM, email, etc.). In these virtual communities, existing members send out messages inviting new people to become members of their personal networks. New members repeat the process, growing the total number of members in the social network. These online services typically offer automatic address book updates, and viewable persona profiles. Popular examples include: Facebook <http://www.facebook.com/>, MySpace <http://www.myspace. com/>, Bebo <http://www.bebo.com/>, and MSN Spaces <http://spaces.msn.com/>. Many social networking services are also blog hosting services. Social networking sites have millions of regular users each.
- A podcast is an audio or audio/video broadcast, with new episodes released either sporadically or at planned intervals such as daily or weekly. Examples include talk radio programs, news shows, short films, lectures, and stories. Podcasting is a method of distributing multimedia files, such as audio programs or music videos, over the Internet using various syndication formats, for playback on mobile devices and personal computers. More than 22 million American adults own iPods or MP3 players and 29% of them have downloaded podcasts from the Web.[24]
- Content systems are online publishing systems for text or media files. The software controls access and helps end users organize and disseminate their posted content. Courseware systems like Blackboard and WebCT are educational examples of content systems.
- Listservs are electronic mailing list software applications.

Embedded, intentionally or unintentionally, are referrals to specific sources–products and services. The amount of WOM marketing activity going on is astounding. In 2006, for example, a 17-year-old youth shot a relationship breakup video, uploaded it to YouTube.com and it was viewed more than 300,000 times in two weeks.[25] The video helped introduce Logitech Web cameras to scores of young people. Sales spiked high enough for Logitech to notice.

ERESOURCE MARKETING CAMPAIGNS

It is difficult for libraries, most of which continue to have a physical existence, to move away from a "library as place" marketing mindset. They've invested in their online portals and seek traffic to justify their investment. Library awareness marketing goals routinely overshadow specific resource and search service awareness goals. There is a focus on the "'whole" over the "parts." Unfortunately, most users will only gravitate to a portal after its resources have demonstrated value to them. Direct access to a library's resources, from a user's regularly-visited Web sites, allows users to sample context-sensitive digital library holdings at their point of need or their familiar online place.

Online traffic follows a network of connections through hyperlinks between outside information resources and the library's digital holdings and online search services. It is hard to accept that the whole is no longer greater than the sum of its parts. Libraries cannot expect to stay popular all the time in an ever-shifting information environment. They can, however, try to get their resources listed at currently popular online, to drive traffic to their resources. A library's resources will always be fresher than its brand. Front door library Web site traffic will, in time, follow the upward traffic trends of usage of specific library resources. The same online traffic goal is realized; just a different strategy is used to achieve it.

ESTABLISHING ORGANIZATIONAL MARKETING GOALS AND OBJECTIVES

Annual goals and objectives statements are required by management in many organizations. If a library is considering implementation of a WOM referral marketing campaign, setting goals and objectives is an important step in the process. Goals are broad, general intentions; they are often intangible and cannot be easily measured. Objectives are the deliverables that will be used to meet a specific goal. They are precise, tangible, and measurable. The accomplishment of the objective can be observed and measured. Measurement can be as easy as pass/fail or a percentage that is known to be completed. For example: a library's goals and objectives for marketing electronic resources may include the following.

Goal #1: Increase Awareness of the Library's Licensed Online Resources

Objective #1: Develop and deploy an electronic resources survey instrument.

Objective #2: Provide the editors of 20 academic department Web sites with an annotated and hyperlinked list of relevant information products, licensed by the library. Negotiate the posting of the list to the department's Web site.

Objective #3: Provide the editors of 10 community group Web sites with an annotated and hyperlinked list of relevant information products, licensed by the library. Negotiate the posting of the list to each group's Web site.

Objective #4: Plan and deliver a "brown bag" digital library orientation luncheon, for middle school teachers, on a pedagogical day, at the local middle school.

Objective #5: Decrease interlibrary loan requests by 10% for materials available online.

Objective #6: Acquire and deploy a full-text "link resolver."

Objective #7: Acquire a "federated search engine" for the library's digital holdings.

Goal #2: Increase Usage of the Library's Licensed Online Resources

Objective #1: Increase the number of full-text articles downloaded by 10%.

Objective #2: Identify the bottom 10%, measured by usage (searches, fulltext downloads, etc.) of the library's e-journal databases. Arrange one-on-one meetings with 3 potential users for each product. Ask them for the names of two friends or acquaintances who might also be interested in the products. Arrange one-on-one meetings with the new contacts.

Objective #3: License and setup remote access to the top 10 information products, by usage, currently unavailable remotely.
Objective #4: Double the number of "concurrent users" on the top 5 information products, measured by "turnaways."
Objective #5: Increase the number of course assignment based information literacy classes offered by 20%.

IDENTIFYING TARGET MARKETS

Marketing campaigns target specific groups of people. Ideally, to maximize effectiveness, the defined groups should be known to be both reachable and responsive. Target groups can be the library's strongest user base, weakest user base, least satisfied user group, the user group with the highest unrealized potential for digital library usage, undergraduates in subject disciplines requiring heavy research activity, graduate students, international students, ESL readers, community groups, etc. The challenge for libraries doing WOM marketing is how to identify influential online speakers, in each target group in the community to contact. The objective is to have these speakers provide both online (via blogs, Web sites, podcasts, etc.) and face-to-face referrals to specific library resources. This point is important because a recent study suggests 92% of WOM marketing happens offline.[26] These writers will both talk up the resources with their social groups and populate resource links across popular community Web sites, to enable others to do the same, to a degree library staff never could.

Malcolm Gladwell, author of the *Tipping Point: How Little Things Can Make a Big Difference*,[27] and Emanuel Rosen, author of *Anatomy of Buzz: How to Create Word of Mouth Marketing*,[28] give insight into identifying influential speakers to target for WOM marketing campaigns. Gladwell talks about influential people falling into two categories: "Mavens" and "Connectors." Connectors are people who know a lot of people and keep in touch. They have a special gift for bringing the world together.[29] Six degrees of separation doesn't mean that everyone is linked to everyone else in just 6 steps. "It means that a very few number of people are linked to everyone else in a few steps and the rest of us are linked to the world through these special few."[30] Mavens are people who possess a wealth of information and are willing and inclined to share it with others. They like to help and they are trusted. They like to initiate discussions with consumers and respond to requests.[31] They are the type of person who writes comments on blog postings and writes letters to the editor to make corrections. Connectors get information from mavens and spread it to large numbers of people.

Emanual Rosen groups influential people into "hubs." Hubs are individuals who communicate with more people about a certain product than the average person does.[32] A "regular hub" is the kind of person who spreads information about a product and influences other people. They can connect to a few people or a few dozen. "Expert hubs" are people who are listened to because they are an authority in a certain field. These are similar to Gladwell's "Mavens." "Social hubs" are the kinds of people who connect with other people and bring people together, similar to Gladwell's "connectors." They are usually ahead in the adoption of new things compared to the majority of people. Rosen characterizes hub people as being very connected (they go to trade shows and belong to user groups and online forums); tend to travel; they are information hungry, they are constantly researching, reading and viewing new content; and they are vocal, they have opinions and share them.

Library staff, and administrative assistants and managers outside the library are primary people to contact for assistance in identifying the target groups' mavens, connectors, and hubs, both on and off site (inside and outside the firm, institution or city department). Alternatively, library communities can be polled to identify influential speakers. Building an initial list of people to contact with online influence for WOM marketing is relatively easy; fleshing it out is hard. It can take years to have a complete picture in a large organization; all the while people join and leave the organization and its external contacts. Building relationships with people and gaining their trust takes time. Some people will never be reachable and/or responsive to product placement or referral requests. Ideally you seek people who can pass along your messages without need for more than an initial stimulus, are able to replicate the message without loss of content, and can manage the speed and direction of transmission of your messages.[33] There will be a mix of WOM home runs and foul balls. Target markets will change from year to year, but the foundation will always be there if you regularly nurture it. WOM speakers have to have an incentive to stay on the payroll, so to speak. The reward for performance is being kept "in-the-know," something they value. Talk to them frequently and regularly, pass along fresh content as soon as it becomes available. Nurture their need.

NECESSITY OF PURLs

While early digital library resources lacked static hyperlink function-ality, a necessity for referral WOM marketing, persistent URLs are be-coming ubiquitous in licensed digital library resources. Persistent links provide an advantage over the standard copy-and-paste Web browser address bar links because they are stable, or persistent, over time. Web browser address links are often search-session specific and become non-functional in a short period of time. You can create direct links to a variety of online content such as:

- Full-text articles and citations from newspapers, magazines, jour-nals or reference works.
- Periodical (journal, magazine, newspaper) titles (title level access).
- Full-text books.
- User-defined searches (a link that launches a pre-defined search which retrieves "fresh hits" each time it is clicked).
- Specific databases.
- Library catalogue records (direct links to holdings information for items held in the library).

The links are becoming easier to locate or build. Staff involved in WOM marketing need to provide instruction to targeted individuals and groups on capabilities of persistent hyperlinks and how they can be uti-lized to share resources with their communities. Based on experience, the average Web content developer or browser tries to cut-and-paste a link from the Web browser window or by "right clicking" over the hyperlink in an Windows environment, and selecting "copy shortcut" from the menu that appears. They then test the link. If it works, great; if not, they move, on assuming the Web address (Web site, database, e-journal, e-book, image, etc.) cannot be bookmarked. The persistent Web address (PURL) is often available somewhere on the page or by editing the browser hyperlink. Once you've done it a few times, it be-comes second nature.

For WOM to be successful, from an online conversation standpoint (blogs, podcasts, etc.), the speaker must be able to communicate the PURL for the resource they are discussing. Some secondary and higher education institutions are permitting library staff to gain access to a course's online resource postings on courseware systems so library staff can insert hyperlinks to required and supplemental resources. Given the reality that many people tune out when faced with technical instructions, providing WOM speakers with content they can cut-and-paste or edit, is key for success. After conversing with a community member about a specific resource licensed by the library, it is helpful to send the PURL for the resource and a brief blurb about it to the person so they can more easily share it with others, whether online, by copying, or face-to-face. Editable cut-and-paste samples include:

> Here is a follow up to what we talked about in the hall last night: Seneca Libraries has migrated access to Canadian Encyclopedic Digest and Canadian Case Digests from CDROM's installed on Computing Commons workstations to web access. The following products are now available via LawSource <http://library.senecac. on.ca/resources/carswellCCD.html>: Canadian Abridgements eDigest (SDI); Index to Canadian Legal Literature; Canadian Abridgement; Case Law, Legislation; Canadian Abridgement Case Digests; Canadian Encyclopedic Digest; Carswell Law Report Articles; Journals and Law Reviews; and KeyCite Canada. A training announcement will be sent out in the next few weeks.

> Syndetic Solutions
> The information available for decision making in our library catalogue is disappointingly sparse, compared to experiences of searching in today's information rich, visually oriented online bookstore catalogues (Amazon.com, Indigochapters.ca). To bridge the gap, we have initiated a subscription to Syndetics Solution, to enhance the information available in our catalogue's bibliographic records. Enhanced content can include: book cover images, fiction profiles, author biographies, extensive tables of contents, book reviews, excerpts, book summaries and first chapters. Content varies by title, and at least half of last year's acquisitions have "some" enhanced content available. Look for an "Additional Information" hyperlink on library catalogue record displays.

> New Embargos for Canadian Newstand <http://library.senecac. on.ca/resources/bh_cdnnews.html> Canadian Newsstand which offers access to the full text of over 190 Canadian news sources from Canada's newspaper publishers is now even more current! The previous seven-day embargo on content is now reduced to 48 hours.

Databases with Content Delivery Options (SDI)
Did you know that many of our subscription databases have 'selective dissemination of information' (SDI's) feature sets? Examples include Global Books in Print, ScienceDirect, EBSCO, ACM Digital Library and ProQuest. In essence, you pre-select content you want to stay current with and it is 'pushed' to you, through email, on a monthly basis. Content delivery possibilities include: table of contents for each published journal issue or volume, citation retrievals from pre-set research queries and citation tracking (i.e. tracking articles that cite a specific article). Global Books in Print Alerts are especially helpful to keep on top of book publishing in your collection development areas. For more information see <http://library.senecacollege.ca/Find_Articles/Alerts/index.html>

To disseminate these types of digital library resource "tidbits" to your community of bloggers and blog readers (your WOM community speakers) on a regular basis, blog syndication technologies like RSS and ATOM, enable WOM library marketing staff to "push" content, on a regular basis. RSS (Really Simple Syndication) and ATOM are a technology for pushing headlines and other Web content to subscribers, largely from blogs, thereby bypassing the need to visit a site on a regular basis. The content comes to you instead of you going to it.

Programs are available that display multiple RSS or ATOM feeds in a single interface. Blog feeds are an easy way for librarians and library patrons to create in-context, links to licensed digital library content at the point of need. It enables the easy integration of library resources into already popular Web sites; unlike persistent links copied or built from database record data, which require consulting with product service manuals or in library training, RSS/ATOM is already widely adopted and in use by Web content developers. In essence it makes referral marketing easy. The WOM marketing results sought cannot be achieved with a general library news type blog. Each target market needs its own blog. By experience, people treat uninteresting pushed content as spam. The "tidbits" need to be focused to each speaker's direct interests. Otherwise you are just pushing spam and annoying them.

CAMPAIGN EVALUATION

A "return on investment" mindset is beginning to gain traction in libraries that have a strong culture of assessment. Evaluating the achievement of goals and objectives by collecting and interpreting evidence is rapidly becoming standard professional practice. There is no sense in conducting marketing activities if you have no plans for assessment or are unable to measure results. You need to know what your return on investment was before you allocate resources to do it again. You need to know what actions were successful and which were not to ensure resources (staff time, funding, etc.) are not squandered needlessly and problems can be identified for resolution.

Many libraries market themselves without knowing if it is having any effect whatsoever. It just becomes something else you do because everyone else is doing it. It sounds great in theory. In this fiscally challenging era of libraries, this approach to marketing is reckless. Marketing goals for a campaign need to be supported by measurable objectives. Each pre-established objective supporting each marketing goal is evaluated along the lines of pass/fail. Either the objective was met or it was not. Based on these findings, the campaign's goals are evaluated in terms of success and failure. A clear picture of the outcomes of the WOM/referral marketing initiatives is available if this type of assessment is conducted. You will have an answer to the questions: was the library successful in getting some of its resources "Slashdotted" by influential speakers in the community? Is the library plugged into the new engine for growth: "the spare cycles, talent and capacity of regular folks, who are, in aggregate, creating a distributed labor force of unprecedented scale?"[34]

CONCLUSION

The consumer adoption of the Internet, as a content and communication medium, has libraries competing for traffic with a constantly growing list of competitors, many of which are considerably better funded. In this unimaginably large information and content universe, however, the playing field is level, from a marketing perspective. Massive funding does not equal success. Superior design and development does not equal success. The sheer number of people referring others to your online space determines whether you succeed of fail. The rise of MySpace, YouTube and Flickr shows how WOM can channel the online masses to a specific online resource by "Slashdotting" them. Increasing the "echo rate" of your marketing messages online, via blogs, podcasts, Web sites and face-to-face encounters does not require big publication budgets, only library staff talking to the right people in their community, on a regular basis. WOM marketing is an increasingly effective marketing communications strategy in an era whereby interpersonal communications technologies dominate the traditional mass media in influence over consumers.[35] WOM marketing challenges the cost argument used by so many libraries, as to why they do not do much marketing of their products and services. Declining or stagnant customer bases don't bode well for continued library funding. Libraries cannot afford not to market.

NOTES

1. Association of Research Libraries. *ARL Statistics 2003-2004. Service Trends in ARL Libraries, 1991-2004* (Washington, DC: ARL Publications Program, 2005), http://www.arl.org/stats/arlstat/graphs/2004/pubser04.pdf (accessed October 5, 2006).

2. OCLC. *Perceptions of Libraries and Information Resources: a Report to the OCLC Membership* (Dublin, OH: Online Computer Library Center Inc., 2005), http://www.oclc.org/reports/2005perceptions.htm (accessed October 6, 2006).

3. Naqvi, Zafar Javed. 2004. "Marketing of Information Products and Services for Libraries." *Pakistan Library and Information Science Journal* 35:1-8.

4. Lindgaard, G., G. Fernandes., C. Dudek and J. Brown. 2006. "Attention web designers: you have 50 milliseconds to make a good first impression!" *Behaviour & Information Technology* 25:115-126.

5. OCLC.

6. Bennett, Julie. "New World of Marketing: Word-of-Mouth Campaigns Replace Traditional Tools." *Wall Street Journal* (February 7, 2006):B7.

7. Datta, Palto R., Chowdhury, Dababrata N., & Bonya R. Chakraborty. 2005. "Viral Marketing: New Form of Word-of-Mouth Through the Internet." *Business Review* 3: 69-75.

8. Bone, P.F. 1992. "Determinants of Word-of-Mouth Communications During Product Consumption." *Advances in Consumer Research* 14: 350-362.

9. Carl, Walter J. 2006. "What's All The Buzz About? Everyday Communication and The Relational Basis of Word-of-Mouth and Buzz Marketing Practices." *Management Communication Quarterly* 19: 601-634.

10. Torio, James. "Blogs: A Global Conversation." (masters thesis, SUNY Stonybrook), 2005, http://www.everyhuman.com/work/theses8.12.low.pdf (accessed October 5, 2006).

11. Datta.

12. George Silverman, *Secrets of Word of Mouth Advertising* (New York: Amacom, 2001).

13. Torio.

14. Bennett.

15. Silverman.

16. Datta.

17. Stabb, Steffen. "Social Networks Applied." *IEEE Intelligent Systems* 20 (1): 80-93.

18. OCLC.

19. Terveen, Loren and Will Hill. "Beyond Recommender Systems: Helping People Help Each Other." In Jack Carroll (ed.) *Human-Computer Interaction in the New Millennium* (Boston: ACM Press, 2001).

20. David, Shay and Trevor Pinch. 2006. "Six degrees of Reputation: the use and abuse of online recommendation systems." *First Monday* 11 (3) http://www.firstmonday.org/issues/issue11_3/david/index.html (accessed October 4, 2006).

21. Masum, Hassan and Yi-Cheng Zhang. 2004. "Manifesto for the Reputation Society." *First Monday* 9 (7) http://firstmonday.org/issues/issue9_7/masum/index.html (accessed October 4, 2006).

22. Pew Internet & American Life Project. *State of Blogging*. Washington, DC: Pew Internet & American Life Project, 2005. http://www.pewinternet.org/PPF/r/144/report_display.asp (accessed October 6, 2006).

23. Torio.

24. Pew.

25. Sandoval, Greg. "Teen Filmmaker Attracts Logitech's Focus." *C|NET News. com*, March 27, 2006 http://news.com.com/Teen+filmmaker+attracts+Logitechs+focus/2100-1025_3-6054602.html (accessed October 7, 2007).

26. Wojnicki, Andrea. "Online vs Offline WOM–Are the Differences a Big Deal?" *WOMMA Research Blog* http://www.womma.org/research/online_vs_offli.htm (accessed October 8, 2006).

27. Gladwell, Malcolm. *Tipping Point: How Little Things Can Make a Big Difference* (New York: Back Bay Books, 2000).

28. Rosen, Emanuel. *Anatomy of Buzz: How to Create Word of Mouth Marketing* (New York: Currency, 2000).

29. Gladwell.

30. Gladwell, 36.

31. Gladwell.

32. Rosen.

33. Alexander, Peter. "Electronic Word-of-Mouth Communication: Factors That Influence the Forwarding of E-Mail Messages." (Ph.D. Dissertation, Touro University International), 2006, http://www.womma.org/content/Pete-Alexander-Dissertation-Writeup-Publication.pdf (accessed October 5, 2006).

34. Anderson, Chris. "People Power: Blogs, User Reviews, Photo-Sharing-the Peer Production Era Has Arrived." *Wired* (July 2006) http://www.wired.com/wired/archive/14.07/people.html (accessed October 7, 2006).

35. Alexander.

Index